THE STATE OF GERMANY ATLAS

Bernhard Schäfers is a political scientist who was born in 1939. He has been Professor of Sociology and Director of the Institute of Sociology at the University of Karlsruhe, Baden-Württemberg, since 1983. In 1991-92, he was chair of the *Deutschen Gesellschaft für Soziologie*. He is a member of the *Deutschen Akademie für Städtebau und Landesplanung* and a corresponding member of the *Akademie für Raumforschung und Landesplanung*.

THE STATE OF GERMANY ATLAS

Bernhard Schäfers

with
Yvonne Bernart, Simone Farys
Nicole Hägele, Roger Häußling

London and New York

Originally published in German in 1997
by Verlag J.H.W. Dietz Nachfolger
In der Raste 2, D-53129 Bonn, Germany

First published in English in 1998
by Routledge
11 New Fetter Lane, London EC4P 4EE

Simultaneously published in the USA and Canada
by Routledge
29 West 35th Street, New York, NY 10001

Translated and produced by Myriad Editions Limited,
52 Maple Street, London W1P 5GE

Graphic design by Corinne Pearlman
Maps by All Terrain Mapping
Printed and bound in China by Phoenix Offset

British Library Cataloguing in Publication Data
A catalogue record for this book is available from the
British Library

Library of Congress Cataloging in Publication Data
A catalog record for this book is available from the
Library of Congress

ISBN 0-415-18826-1

CONTENTS

MAJOR SOURCES

The following works are cited in the maps section, in the abbreviated form given at the end of each entry below.

Bundesministerium für Bildung, *Wissenschaft, Forschung und Technologie, Grund- und Strukturdaten 1995/96*, Bonn, December 1995. (Bundesmin. für Bildung)

Eurostat, *Statistische Grundzahlen der Europäischen Union*, Brussels, Luxembourg, 1995, 32nd edition. (Eurostat)

Der Fischer-Weltalmanach: Zahlen, Daten, Fakten '97, Frankfurt am Main, Fischer Taschenbuch Verlag, November 1996. (*Fischer Weltalmanach '97*)

Globus Kartendienst GmbH, Hamburg. (Globus)

Harenberg Kompaktlexikon, Dortmund, 1996, 3 vols. (*Harenberg Lexikon 1996*)

Harenberg Lexikon der Gegenwart: Aktuell '97, Dortmund, 1996. (*Harenberg Aktuell '97*)

Hauchler, Ingomar, ed., *Globale Trends 1996: Fakten, Analysen, Prognosen, Stiftung Entwicklung und Frieden*, Frankfurt am Main, Fischer Taschenbuch Verlag, November 1995. (*Globale Trends 1996*)

Institut der deutschen Wirtschaft Köln, *Zahlen zur wirtschaftlichen Entwicklung der Bundesrepublik Deutschland*, Cologne, various years. (Inst. d. dt. Wirtschaft o. Zahlen)

Jahrbuch der Bundesrepublik Deutschland, by Horst-Hennek Rohlfs and Ursel Schäfer, Frankfurt am Main, 1996, 11th edition. (*Jahrbuch der Br.* 1996)

Schäfers, Bernhard, *Gesellschaftlicher Wandel in Deutschland: Ein Studienbuch zur Sozialstruktur und Sozialgeschichte*, Stuttgart, 1995, 6th revised edition.

Statistisches Bundesamt, *Statistisches Jahrbuch für die Bundesrepublik Deutschland*, Wiesbaden, various years. (*Stat. Jb.*)

Statistisches Bundesamt, *Statistisches Jahrbuch für das Ausland*, 1996, Wiesbaden, 1996. (*Stat. Jb. Ausl.* 1996)

Statistisches Bundesamt, *Bevölkerung und Wirtschaft 1872-1972*, Stuttgart, Mainz, 1972.

Statistisches Bundesamt, *Wirtschaft und Statistik*, various years. (*Wirtschaft und Statistik*)

Statistisches Bundesamt with Wissenschaftszentrum Berlin für Sozialforschung and Zentrum für Umfragen, Methoden und Analysen, Mannheim (ZUMA), *Datenreport 1994: Zahlen und Fakten über die Bundesrepublik Deutschland*, Bundeszentrale für politische Bildung, Bonn 1994, new edition 1995 (*Datenreport*)

Statistisches Amt der Europäischen Gemeinschaft (Eurostat), *Europa in Zahlen*, Brussels, Luxembourg 1995, 4th edition. (*Europa in Zahlen*)

The State of Germany Atlas provides an informative picture of Germany's people, society, economy and political system at the end of the 20th century. Almost every map compares Germany with its 15 partners in the European Union, and sometimes with other major states such as the USA and Japan.

On 3 October 1990, two German states, the Federal Republic of Germany (West Germany) and the German Democratic Republic (East Germany), were unified as a single federal republic. The maps and graphics in this atlas show clearly, sometimes dramatically, how the old, western Länder and new, eastern Länder are still in the process of integration and assimilation.

The eastern Länder were soon able to take on the legal framework, institutions and economic structure of the Federal Republic, but to create a comparable standard of living is taking far longer than was ever imagined. In the early years after unification, the need of the new Länder to improve their productivity and infrastructure were perceived as 'retrospective modernization'. Such a notion, however, did not allow for further ongoing change within Germany as a whole. It has been necessary not only to make up for lost time in the new Länder, but also necessary for the new Federal Republic to respond to other, general social change.

We hope that this atlas provides a reliable, fast and useful source of reference and information and that it will be used by many.

Bernhard Schäfers
Institute of Sociology
University of Karlsruhe

Acknowledgements

The final product cannot really convey how much work and excitement went into its creation. Some 700 pages of data and text were condensed into 128 printed pages. I have been grateful for the commitment of Christine Buchheit, of Verlag J.H.W. Dietz in Bonn, and Anne Benewick, of Myriad Editions in London, in enabling us to meet our deadlines. The statistics were mainly submitted by the colleagues named on the title page of the atlas.We are indebted to many individuals and institutions for their help and support. The latter are fully listed in the sources in the text, although the Federal Statistical Office deserves its own special thanks.

Thanks are also due to two student research assistants, Sabina Misoch and Jennifer Stiebel, as well as Barbara Kupferschmidt and Ilse Willin in the secretary's office at the Institute of Sociology, University of Karlsruhe.

I would also like to thank Gunter E. Zimmermann for his assistance and many useful hints.

Part One

PEOPLE

Source: Stat. Bundesamt

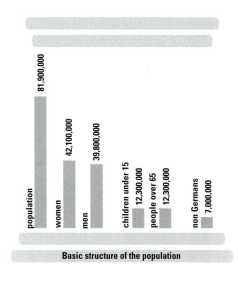

Basic structure of the population

population 81,900,000
women 42,100,000
men 39,800,000
children under 15 12,300,000
people over 65 12,300,000
non Germans 7,000,000

Bernhard Schäfers *The State of Germany Atlas* Copyright © Myriad Editions Limited

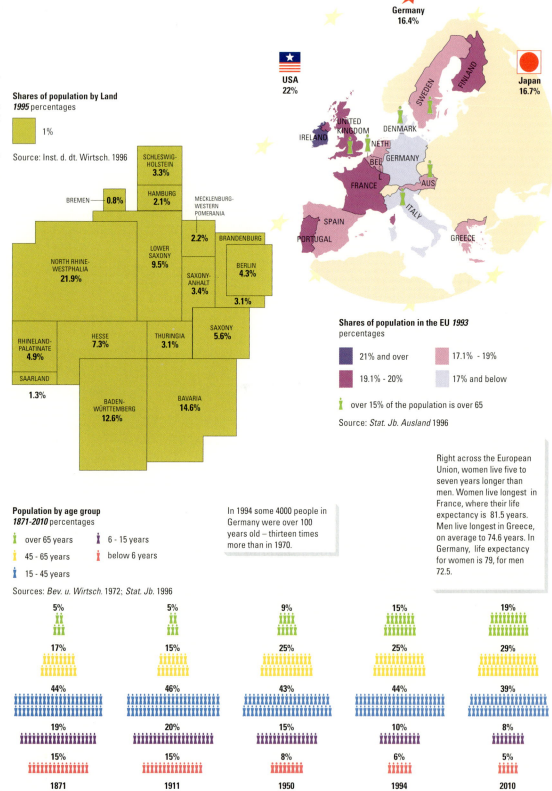

Shares of population by Land
1995 percentages

☐ 1%

Source: Inst. d. dt. Wirtsch. 1996

SCHLESWIG-HOLSTEIN
3.3%

BREMEN **0.8%**

HAMBURG
2.1%

MECKLENBURG-WESTERN POMERANIA
2.2%

BRANDENBURG

NORTH RHINE-WESTPHALIA
21.9%

LOWER SAXONY
9.5%

SAXONY-ANHALT
3.4%

BERLIN
4.3%

3.1%

RHINELAND-PALATINATE
4.9%

HESSE
7.3%

THURINGIA
3.1%

SAXONY
5.6%

SAARLAND

1.3%

BADEN-WÜRTTEMBERG
12.6%

BAVARIA
14.6%

Germany
16.4%

USA
22%

Japan
16.7%

SWEDEN
FINLAND
IRELAND
UNITED KINGDOM
DENMARK
NETH
BEL
GERMANY
L
FRANCE
AUS
ITALY
SPAIN
PORTUGAL
GREECE

Shares of population in the EU *1993*
percentages

☐ 21% and over   ☐ 17.1% - 19%

☐ 19.1% - 20%   ☐ 17% and below

🧍 over 15% of the population is over 65

Source: *Stat. Jb. Ausland* 1996

Right across the European Union, women live five to seven years longer than men. Women live longest in France, where their life expectancy is 81.5 years. Men live longest in Greece, on average to 74.6 years. In Germany, life expectancy for women is 79, for men 72.5.

Population by age group
1871-2010 percentages

🧍 over 65 years   🧍 6 - 15 years

🧍 45 - 65 years   🧍 below 6 years

🧍 15 - 45 years

Sources: *Bev. u. Wirtsch.* 1972; *Stat. Jb.* 1996

In 1994 some 4000 people in Germany were over 100 years old – thirteen times more than in 1970.

	1871	1911	1950	1994	2010
over 65 years	5%	5%	9%	15%	19%
45 - 65 years	17%	15%	25%	25%	29%
15 - 45 years	44%	46%	43%	44%	39%
6 - 15 years	19%	20%	15%	10%	8%
below 6 years	15%	15%	8%	6%	5%

In 1990, unification brought East Germany, with 17 million people, together with a West German population more than three times its size.

Throughout the 1970s and 1980s, East and West Germany had the lowest birth rates in the world. Since the 1990s, the birth rate in Italy has been lower than in Germany, and it has been almost as low in Greece and Spain.

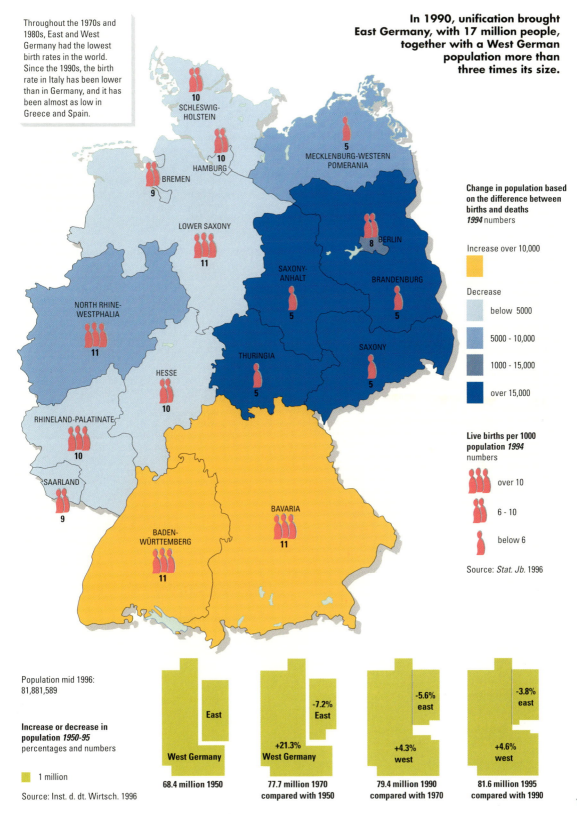

SCHLESWIG-HOLSTEIN
10

HAMBURG
10

BREMEN
9

MECKLENBURG-WESTERN POMERANIA
5

LOWER SAXONY
11

BERLIN
8

SAXONY-ANHALT
5

BRANDENBURG
5

NORTH RHINE-WESTPHALIA
11

HESSE
10

THURINGIA
5

SAXONY
5

RHINELAND-PALATINATE
10

SAARLAND
9

BADEN-WÜRTTEMBERG
11

BAVARIA
11

Change in population based on the difference between births and deaths
1994 numbers

Increase over 10,000

Decrease

below 5000

5000 - 10,000

1000 - 15,000

over 15,000

Live births per 1000 population *1994*
numbers

over 10

6 - 10

below 6

Source: *Stat. Jb.* 1996

Population mid 1996:
81,881,589

Increase or decrease in population *1950-95*
percentages and numbers

1 million

Source: Inst. d. dt. Wirtsch. 1996

East

West Germany

68.4 million 1950

-7.2%
East

+21.3%
West Germany

77.7 million 1970
compared with 1950

-5.6%
east

+4.3%
west

79.4 million 1990
compared with 1970

-3.8%
east

+4.6%
west

81.6 million 1995
compared with 1990

 **PEOPLE**

Couples who cohabit without being married *1990 and 1994*

Source: *Stat.Jb.* 1996

1,658,000

963,000

1990   1994

Marriages and divorces *1950-94*

marriages

divorces

Source: *Stat. Jb. 1996*

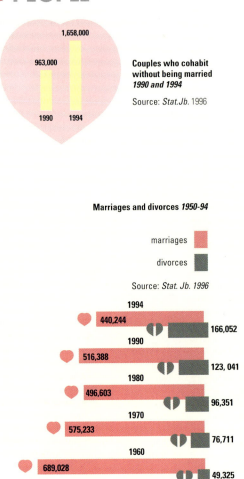

1994
440,244
166,052

1990
516,388
123, 041

1980
496,603
96,351

1970
575,233
76,711

1960
689,028
49,325

1950
750,452
86,341

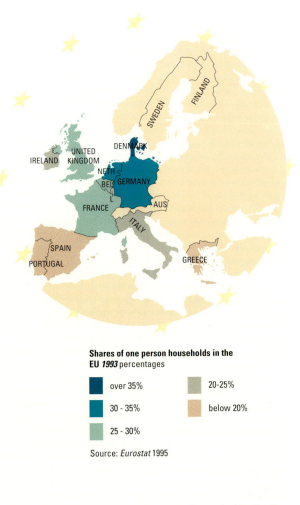

Shares of one person households in the EU *1993* percentages

- over 35%
- 30 - 35%
- 25 - 30%
- 20-25%
- below 20%

Source: *Eurostat* 1995

Changes in size of families *1913-94*

Sources: *Stat. Jb. 1941/42, 1953, 1973, 1983, 1996*

Households *1991*

Source: *Wirtschaft und Statistik* 1993

1%
3 and more generations

7%
single parents

31%
couples with children

24%
one generation

34%
one person households

There are four times as many single mothers with one child as there are single fathers with one child. When more children are involved, they are more likely to live with their single mother . The number of single mothers with three or more children is ten times that of single fathers.

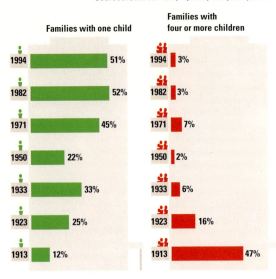

Families with one child

1994 — 51%
1982 — 52%
1971 — 45%
1950 — 22%
1933 — 33%
1923 — 25%
1913 — 12%

Families with four or more children

1994 — 3%
1982 — 3%
1971 — 7%
1950 — 2%
1933 — 6%
1923 — 16%
1913 — 47%

Despite a flourish of alternative forms of family and household, most Germans live within traditional families and marriages.

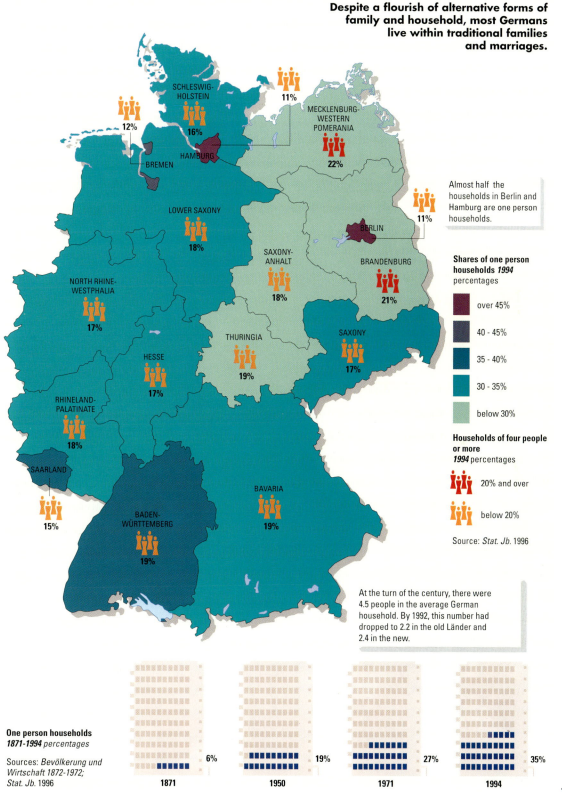

SCHLESWIG-HOLSTEIN
11%

12%

16%

MECKLENBURG-WESTERN POMERANIA

22%

HAMBURG

BREMEN

LOWER SAXONY

18%

11%

BERLIN

Almost half the households in Berlin and Hamburg are one person households.

NORTH RHINE-WESTPHALIA

17%

SAXONY-ANHALT

18%

BRANDENBURG

21%

Shares of one person households *1994* percentages

■ over 45%	
■ 40 - 45%	
■ 35 - 40%	
■ 30 - 35%	
■ below 30%	

HESSE

17%

THURINGIA

19%

SAXONY

17%

RHINELAND-PALATINATE

18%

SAARLAND

15%

BADEN-WÜRTTEMBERG

19%

BAVARIA

19%

Households of four people or more *1994* percentages

👤👤👤 20% and over

👤👤👤 below 20%

Source: *Stat. Jb.* 1996

At the turn of the century, there were 4.5 people in the average German household. By 1992, this number had dropped to 2.2 in the old Länder and 2.4 in the new.

One person households
1871-1994 percentages

Sources: *Bevölkerung und Wirtschaft 1872-1972;*
Stat. Jb. 1996

6%

1871

19%

1950

27%

1971

35%

1994

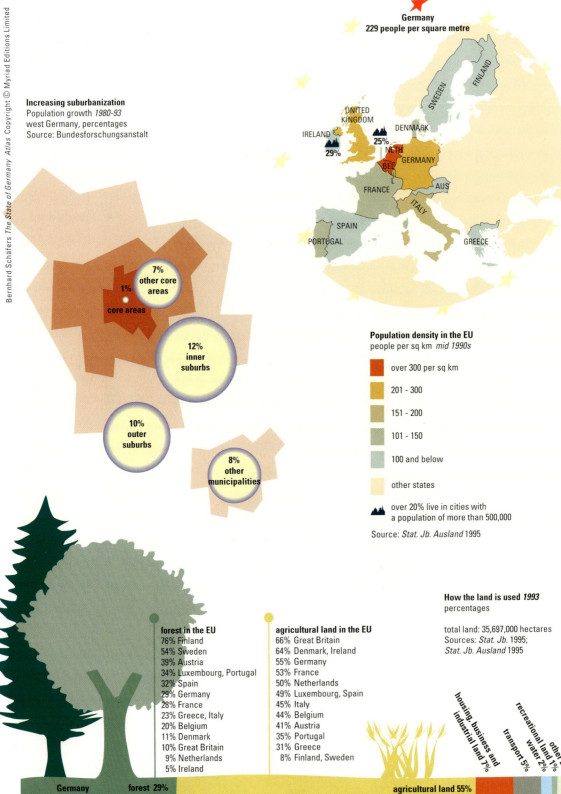

Bernhard Schäfers *The State of Germany Atlas* Copyright © Myriad Editions Limited

Germany
229 people per square metre

Increasing suburbanization
Population growth *1980-93*
west Germany, percentages
Source: Bundesforschungsanstalt

7%
other core
areas

1%
core areas

12%
inner
suburbs

10%
outer
suburbs

8%
other
municipalities

IRELAND
29%

UNITED
KINGDOM

DENMARK
25%

SWEDEN

FINLAND

NETH
BEL
L
FRANCE

GERMANY

AUS

ITALY

SPAIN

PORTUGAL

GREECE

Population density in the EU
people per sq km *mid 1990s*

over 300 per sq km

201 - 300

151 - 200

101 - 150

100 and below

other states

over 20% live in cities with
a population of more than 500,000

Source: *Stat. Jb. Ausland* 1995

forest in the EU
76% Finland
54% Sweden
39% Austria
34% Luxembourg, Portugal
32% Spain
29% Germany
28% France
23% Greece, Italy
20% Belgium
11% Denmark
10% Great Britain
 9% Netherlands
 5% Ireland

agricultural land in the EU
66% Great Britain
64% Denmark, Ireland
55% Germany
53% France
50% Netherlands
49% Luxembourg, Spain
45% Italy
44% Belgium
41% Austria
35% Portugal
31% Greece
 8% Finland, Sweden

How the land is used *1993*
percentages

total land: 35,697,000 hectares
Sources: *Stat. Jb.* 1995;
Stat. Jb. Ausland 1995

housing, business and
industrial land 7%

transport 5%

recreational land 1%

water 2%

other 2%

Germany   **forest 29%**   **agricultural land 55%**

Towns and cities are evenly spread throughout Germany although city regions like the Rhine-Ruhr, with a population of 5.3 million, are beginning to emerge.

Most Germans would like to live in a medium sized town or city.

The densely populated Rhine-Ruhr covers 5000 sq km and has a population of 5.3 million. Before the Second World War, it was one of the world's largest industrial heartlands, and was shaped by its steel and coal industries.

Population density *1995*
people per sq km

- over 300 per sq km
- 201 - 300
- 151 - 200
- 101 - 150
- 100 and below

Big cities

cities with a population of more than 1 million

cities between 500,000 and 1 million

cities with a population between 250,000 and 500,000

cities with a population between 100,000 and 250,000

Sources: Inst. d. dt. Wirtschaft Köln,
Zahlen z. wirtsch. Entw. 1996; *Stat. Jb.* 1996

32% of Germans live in cities of more than 100,000 people, 15% of these, in cities of more than 500,000. 24% live in small towns or cities with populations between 5000 and 20,000.

Proportion of households who own their own home *1988* percentages

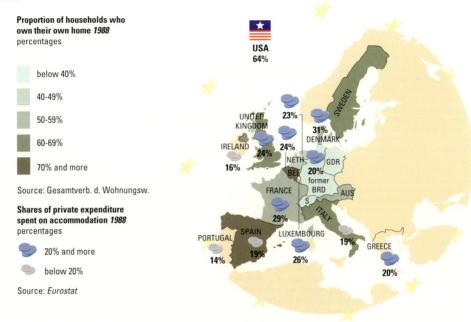

- below 40%
- 40-49%
- 50-59%
- 60-69%
- 70% and more

Source: Gesamtverb. d. Wohnungsw.

Shares of private expenditure spent on accommodation *1988* percentages

- 20% and more
- below 20%

Source: *Eurostat*

USA **64%**

SWEDEN

UNITED KINGDOM **23%**

31% DENMARK

IRELAND **24%**

16%

NETH **24%**

GDR

BEL **20%** former BRD

FRANCE

AUS

S ITALY

29%

PORTUGAL SPAIN LUXEMBOURG

19% GREECE

14% **19%** **26%**

20%

Rent as a proportion of total private expenditure *1994* percentages and in DM per household and month

west ◀ ▶ east

higher income households

1218 DM | 21% | 13% | 502 DM

medium income

921 DM | 23% | 14% | 470 DM

low income

786 DM | 36% | 19% | 403 DM

Source: *Stat. Jb.* 1995

In 1993, only 9.2% of all flats in the old Länder and 0.25% in the new Länder were privately owned.

In 1994, 32% of newly built flats in the old Länder were privately owned, and 24% in the new.

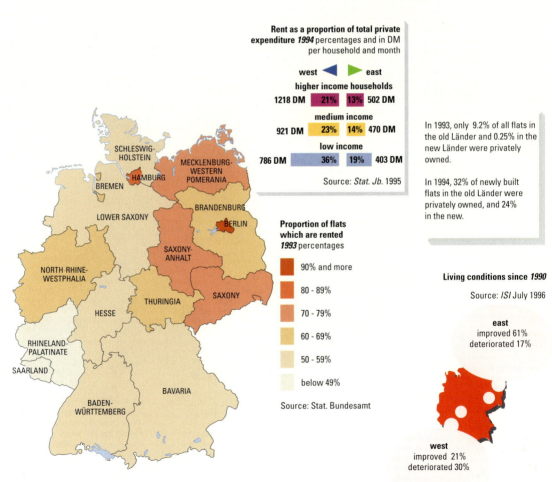

SCHLESWIG-HOLSTEIN

MECKLENBURG-WESTERN POMERANIA

HAMBURG

BREMEN

LOWER SAXONY

BRANDENBURG

BERLIN

SAXONY-ANHALT

NORTH-RHINE-WESTPHALIA

THURINGIA SAXONY

HESSE

RHINELAND-PALATINATE

SAARLAND

BAVARIA

BADEN-WÜRTTEMBERG

Proportion of flats which are rented *1993* percentages

- 90% and more
- 80 - 89%
- 70 - 79%
- 60 - 69%
- 50 - 59%
- below 49%

Source: Stat. Bundesamt

Living conditions since *1990*

Source: *ISI* July 1996

east improved 61% deteriorated 17%

west improved 21% deteriorated 30%

In contrast with the rest of the European Union, Germans tend to rent rather than own their homes.

West Germans have more living space. Half of all homes in the west are larger than 80 square metres, compared with only a third in the east.

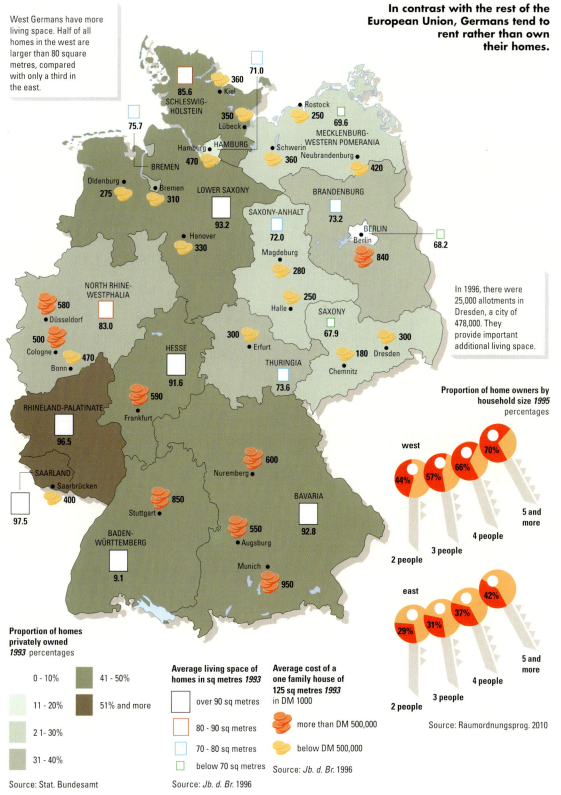

71.0

360
85.6
● Kiel
SCHLESWIG-
HOLSTEIN

350
Lübeck ●

75.7

Hamburg ●
470
HAMBURG

BREMEN

Oldenburg ●
275
● Bremen
310
LOWER SAXONY

93.2

● Hanover

330

NORTH RHINE-
WESTPHALIA

580
● Düsseldorf
83.0

500
Cologne ●
470
Bonn ●

HESSE

91.6

590
Frankfurt ●

RHINELAND-PALATINATE

96.5

SAARLAND
● Saarbrücken
400

97.5

BADEN-
WÜRTTEMBERG

9.1

850
Stuttgart ●

● Rostock
250
69.6
MECKLENBURG-
WESTERN POMERANIA

● Schwerin
360 Neubrandenburg ●
420

BRANDENBURG

73.2

SAXONY-ANHALT

72.0

BERLIN
● Berlin
68.2

840

Magdeburg ●
280

250
Halle ●

SAXONY

67.9

300
● Erfurt

THURINGIA

73.6

180 Dresden ●
300
Chemnitz ●

600
Nuremberg ●

BAVARIA

92.8

550
● Augsburg

Munich ●
950

In 1996, there were 25,000 allotments in Dresden, a city of 478,000. They provide important additional living space.

Proportion of home owners by household size *1995*
percentages

west
44%
57%
66%
70%

2 people
3 people
4 people
5 and more

east
29%
31%
37%
42%

2 people
3 people
4 people
5 and more

Source: Raumordnungsprog. 2010

Proportion of homes privately owned
1993 percentages

0 - 10%	41 - 50%
11 - 20%	51% and more
21- 30%	
31 - 40%	

Source: Stat. Bundesamt

Average living space of homes in sq metres *1993*

□ over 90 sq metres
□ 80 - 90 sq metres
□ 70 - 80 sq metres
□ below 70 sq metres

Source: *Jb. d. Br.* 1996

Average cost of a one family house of 125 sq metres *1993*
in DM 1000

more than DM 500,000

below DM 500,000

Source: *Jb. d. Br.* 1996

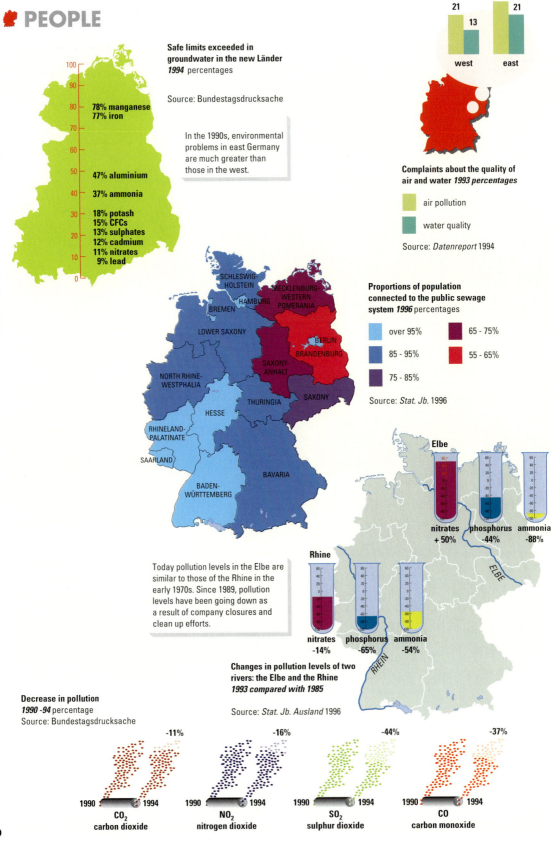

Bernhard Schäfers *The State of Germany Atlas* Copyright © Myriad Editions Limited

Safe limits exceeded in groundwater in the new Länder
1994 percentages

Source: Bundestagsdrucksache

78% manganese
77% iron

47% aluminium

37% ammonia

18% potash
15% CFCs
13% sulphates
12% cadmium
11% nitrates
9% lead

In the 1990s, environmental problems in east Germany are much greater than those in the west.

28
21   21
13

west   east

Complaints about the quality of air and water *1993 percentages*

air pollution

water quality

Source: *Datenreport* 1994

Proportions of population connected to the public sewage system *1996* percentages

over 95%   65 - 75%

85 - 95%   55 - 65%

75 - 85%

Source: *Stat. Jb.* 1996

SCHLESWIG-HOLSTEIN
MECKLENBURG-WESTERN POMERANIA
HAMBURG
BREMEN
LOWER SAXONY
BERLIN
BRANDENBURG
NORTH RHINE-WESTPHALIA
SAXONY-ANHALT
THURINGIA
SAXONY
HESSE
RHINELAND-PALATINATE
SAARLAND
BAVARIA
BADEN-WÜRTTEMBERG

Elbe

nitrates + 50%   phosphorus -44%   ammonia -88%

Rhine

Today pollution levels in the Elbe are similar to those of the Rhine in the early 1970s. Since 1989, pollution levels have been going down as a result of company closures and clean up efforts.

nitrates -14%   phosphorus -65%   ammonia -54%

ELBE

RHEIN

Changes in pollution levels of two rivers: the Elbe and the Rhine *1993 compared with 1985*

Source: *Stat. Jb. Ausland* 1996

Decrease in pollution *1990 -94* percentage
Source: Bundestagsdrucksache

-11%   -16%   -44%   -37%

1990   1994   1990   1994   1990   1994   1990   1994

CO_2 NO_2 SO_2 CO
carbon dioxide   nitrogen dioxide   sulphur dioxide   carbon monoxide

The environment has been a major social and political issue since the 1970s.

In 1995, tree damage was greatest in the forest covered areas of Hesse and Thuringia.

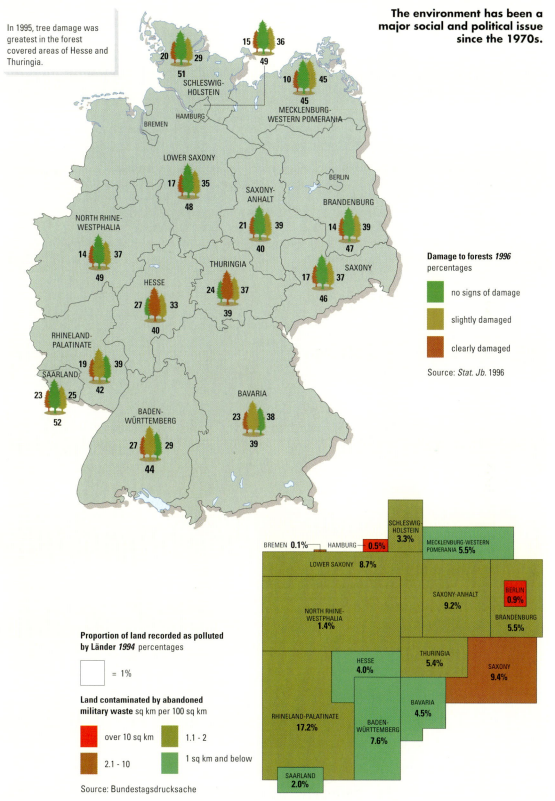

Damage to forests *1996*
percentages

- no signs of damage
- slightly damaged
- clearly damaged

Source: *Stat. Jb.* 1996

SCHLESWIG-HOLSTEIN
15 36
20 29
49
51

MECKLENBURG-WESTERN POMERANIA
10 45
45

HAMBURG

BREMEN

LOWER SAXONY
17 35
48

SAXONY-ANHALT
21 39
40

BERLIN

BRANDENBURG
14 39
47

NORTH RHINE-WESTPHALIA
14 37
49

THURINGIA
24 37
39

SAXONY
17 37
46

HESSE
27 33
40

RHINELAND-PALATINATE
19 39
42

SAARLAND
23 25
52

BADEN-WÜRTTEMBERG
27 29
44

BAVARIA
23 38
39

Proportion of land recorded as polluted by Länder *1994* percentages

☐ = 1%

Land contaminated by abandoned military waste sq km per 100 sq km

- over 10 sq km
- 2.1 - 10
- 1.1 - 2
- 1 sq km and below

Source: Bundestagsdrucksache

BREMEN **0.1%** HAMBURG **0.5%**

SCHLESWIG-HOLSTEIN **3.3%**

MECKLENBURG-WESTERN POMERANIA **5.5%**

LOWER SAXONY **8.7%**

SAXONY-ANHALT **9.2%**

BERLIN **0.9%**

BRANDENBURG **5.5%**

NORTH RHINE-WESTPHALIA **1.4%**

HESSE **4.0%**

THURINGIA **5.4%**

SAXONY **9.4%**

BAVARIA **4.5%**

RHINELAND-PALATINATE **17.2%**

BADEN-WÜRTTEMBERG **7.6%**

SAARLAND **2.0%**

International movement of Germans
1994

→ more returned than left

→ more left than returned

Source: *Stat. Jb.* 1996

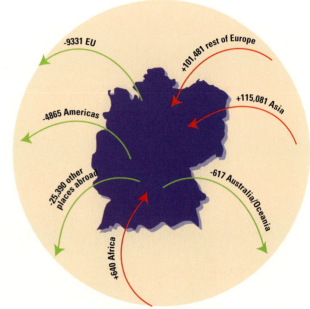

-9331 EU

+101,481 rest of Europe

+115,081 Asia

-4865 Americas

-617 Australia/Oceania

-25,390 other places abroad

+640 Africa

1990 421,947
1980 458,769
1970 495,675
1960 209,978

Numbers who moved away from Germany
1960-90

Sources: *Bevölkerung u. Wirtschaft 1872-1972; Stat. Jb.* 1990

Numbers who moved from East to West *1989-91*
per 1000 population

- over 12
- 8 - 12
- 4 - 8
- below 4

Source: Grundmann 1995

MECKLENBURG-WESTERN POMERANIA
BRANDENBURG
BERLIN (East)
SAXONY-ANHALT
THURINGIA
SAXONY

Movement from the GDR (including East Berlin) into West Germany (including West Berlin)
numbers

- refugees
- immigrants
- released political prisoners

Source: *Deutschland-Archiv* 1989, 1991

One third of the working population commutes between municipalities. 10% go home only at weekends.

The Berlin Wall came down in 1989. In that year alone, 343,854 east Germans moved to the west.

Berlin Wall built 1961

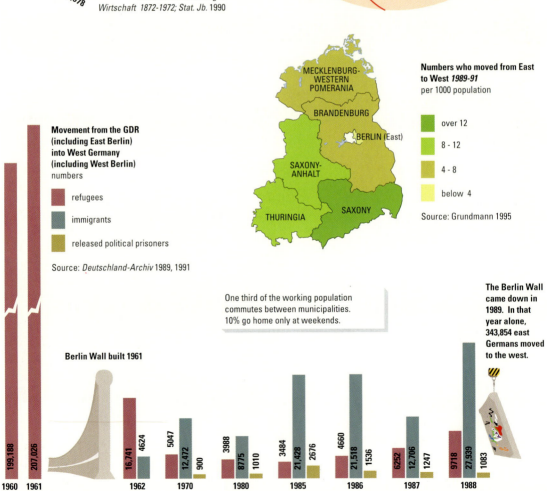

1960	1961	1962	1970	1980	1985	1986	1987	1988
199,188	207,026	16,741 / 4624	5047 / 12,472 / 900	3988 / 8775 / 1010	3484 / 21,428 / 2676	4660 / 21,518 / 1536	6252 / 12,706 / 1247	9718 / 27,939 / 1083

**More people are moving home because people
change jobs more often and because of
regional inequalities.**

Each year, about a million
people move from one
German Land to another.

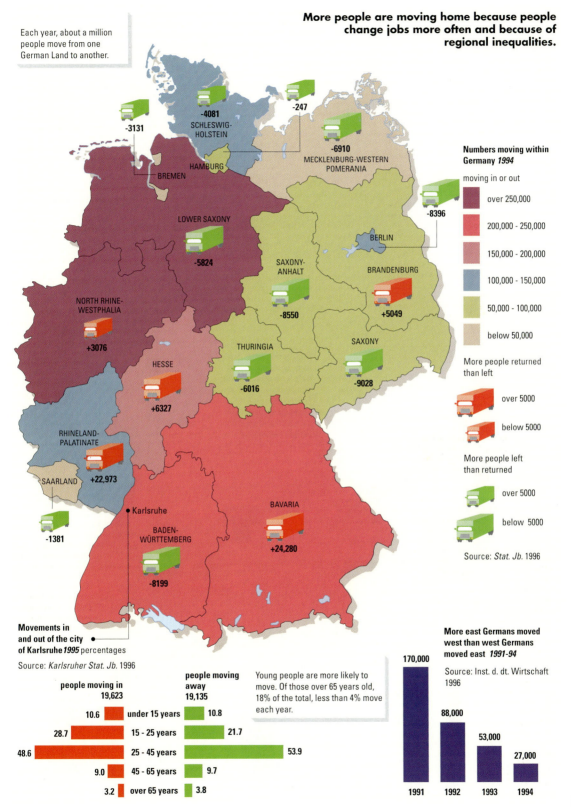

**Numbers moving within
Germany** *1994*

moving in or out

■	over 250,000
■	200,000 - 250,000
■	150,000 - 200,000
■	100,000 - 150,000
■	50,000 - 100,000
■	below 50,000

More people returned
than left

over 5000

below 5000

More people left
than returned

over 5000

below 5000

Source: *Stat. Jb.* 1996

-3131

-4081
SCHLESWIG-
HOLSTEIN

-247

-6910
MECKLENBURG-WESTERN
POMERANIA

HAMBURG

BREMEN

LOWER SAXONY
-5824

-8396

BERLIN

SAXONY-
ANHALT
-8550

BRANDENBURG
+5049

NORTH RHINE-
WESTPHALIA
+3076

HESSE
+6327

THURINGIA
-6016

SAXONY
-9028

RHINELAND-
PALATINATE

+22,973

SAARLAND

-1381

● Karlsruhe

BADEN-
WÜRTTEMBERG
-8199

BAVARIA
+24,280

**Movements in
and out of the city
of Karlsruhe** *1995* percentages

Source: *Karlsruher Stat. Jb.* 1996

people moving in 19,623		people moving away 19,135
10.6	under 15 years	10.8
28.7	15 - 25 years	21.7
48.6	25 - 45 years	53.9
9.0	45 - 65 years	9.7
3.2	over 65 years	3.8

Young people are more likely to
move. Of those over 65 years old,
18% of the total, less than 4% move
each year.

**More east Germans moved
west than west Germans
moved east** *1991-94*

Source: Inst. d. dt. Wirtschaft
1996

170,000	88,000	53,000	27,000
1991	1992	1993	1994

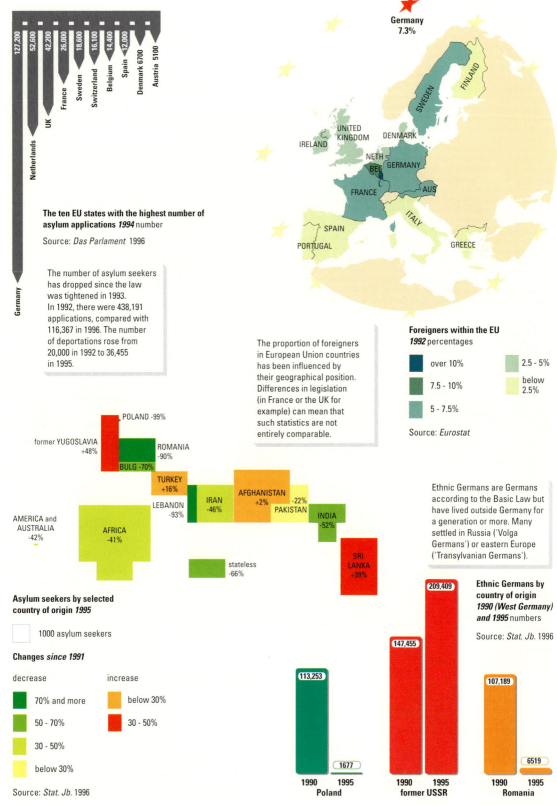

The ten EU states with the highest number of asylum applications *1994* number

Source: *Das Parlament* 1996

Germany 127,200
Netherlands 52,600
UK 42,200
France 26,000
Sweden 18,600
Switzerland 16,100
Belgium 14,400
Spain 12,000
Denmark 6700
Austria 5100

The number of asylum seekers has dropped since the law was tightened in 1993. In 1992, there were 438,191 applications, compared with 116,367 in 1996. The number of deportations rose from 20,000 in 1992 to 36,455 in 1995.

The proportion of foreigners in European Union countries has been influenced by their geographical position. Differences in legislation (in France or the UK for example) can mean that such statistics are not entirely comparable.

Germany 7.3%

Foreigners within the EU
1992 percentages

- over 10%
- 7.5 - 10%
- 5 - 7.5%
- 2.5 - 5%
- below 2.5%

Source: *Eurostat*

Ethnic Germans are Germans according to the Basic Law but have lived outside Germany for a generation or more. Many settled in Russia ('Volga Germans') or eastern Europe ('Transylvanian Germans').

POLAND -99%
former YUGOSLAVIA +48%
ROMANIA -90%
BULG -70%
TURKEY +16%
LEBANON -93%
IRAN -46%
AFGHANISTAN +2%
PAKISTAN -22%
INDIA -52%
AMERICA and AUSTRALIA -42%
AFRICA -41%
stateless -66%
SRI LANKA +39%

Asylum seekers by selected country of origin *1995*

1000 asylum seekers

Changes *since 1991*

decrease
- 70% and more
- 50 - 70%
- 30 - 50%
- below 30%

increase
- below 30%
- 30 - 50%

Source: *Stat. Jb.* 1996

Ethnic Germans by country of origin *1990 (West Germany) and 1995* numbers

Source: *Stat. Jb.* 1996

Poland 1990 113,253 — 1995 1677
former USSR 1990 147,455 — 1995 209,409
Romania 1990 107,189 — 1995 6519

Large numbers of foreign workers, returning ethnic Germans, asylum seekers and political refugees, make Germany a country of immigrants.

For historic reasons, the percentage of non Germans living in the east is much lower than the percentage living in the west..

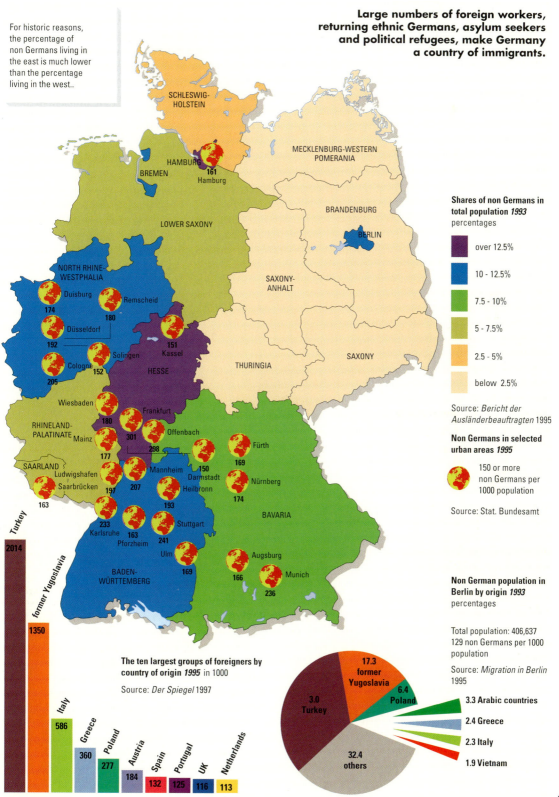

SCHLESWIG-HOLSTEIN

MECKLENBURG-WESTERN POMERANIA

HAMBURG **161** Hamburg

BREMEN

LOWER SAXONY

BRANDENBURG

BERLIN

NORTH RHINE-WESTPHALIA

Duisburg **174**
Remscheid **180**
Düsseldorf **192**
Cologne **205**
Solingen **152**
151 Kassel

HESSE

SAXONY-ANHALT

SAXONY

THURINGIA

Wiesbaden **180**
Frankfurt **301**
Offenbach **298**
Fürth **169**
Mainz **177**
Mannheim **207**
Darmstadt **150**
Nürnberg **174**
Heilbronn **193**

RHINELAND-PALATINATE

SAARLAND
Ludwigshafen **197**
Saarbrücken **163**

Karlsruhe **233**
Pforzheim **163**
Stuttgart **241**
Ulm **169**

BAVARIA

Augsburg **166**
Munich **236**

BADEN-WÜRTTEMBERG

Shares of non Germans in total population *1993* percentages

- over 12.5%
- 10 - 12.5%
- 7.5 - 10%
- 5 - 7.5%
- 2.5 - 5%
- below 2.5%

Source: *Bericht der Ausländerbeauftragten* 1995

Non Germans in selected urban areas *1995*

150 or more non Germans per 1000 population

Source: Stat. Bundesamt

Non German population in Berlin by origin *1993* percentages

Total population: 406,637
129 non Germans per 1000 population

Source: *Migration in Berlin* 1995

The ten largest groups of foreigners by country of origin *1995* in 1000

Source: *Der Spiegel* 1997

Turkey **2014**
former Yugoslavia **1350**
Italy **586**
Greece **360**
Poland **277**
Austria **184**
Spain **132**
Portugal **125**
UK **116**
Netherlands **113**

17.3 former Yugoslavia
6.4 Poland
3.0 Turkey
3.3 Arabic countries
2.4 Greece
2.3 Italy
1.9 Vietnam
32.4 others

Part Two

SOCIETY

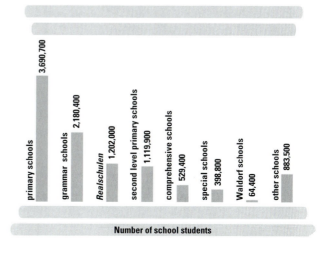

primary schools — 3,690,700

grammar schools — 2,180,400

Realschulen — 1,202,000

second level primary schools — 1,119,900

comprehensive schools — 529,400

special schools — 398,800

Waldorf schools — 64,400

other schools — 883,500

Number of school students

Source: Globus 3988/1997

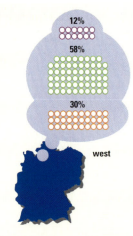

How people perceive their own social position, west Germany *1994*

Source: Noll 1995

- ○ upper class and upper middle class
- ○ middle class
- ○ lower and working class

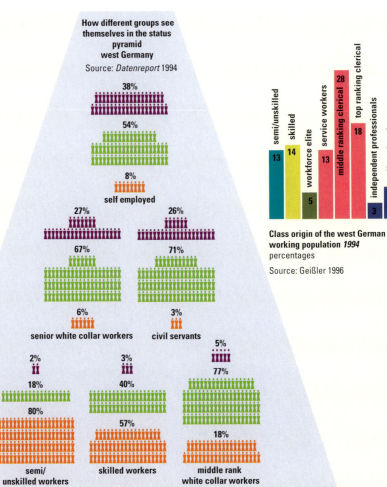

How different groups see themselves in the status pyramid west Germany

Source: *Datenreport* 1994

38%
54%
8%
self employed

27%   26%
67%   71%
6%   3%
senior white collar workers   **civil servants**

2%   3%   5%
18%   40%   77%
80%   57%   18%
semi/ unskilled workers   **skilled workers**   **middle rank white collar workers**

Class origin of the west German working population *1994*
percentages

Source: Geißler 1996

semi/unskilled	13
skilled	14
workforce elite	5
service workers	13
middle ranking clerical	28
top ranking clerical	18
independent professionals	3
self employed	6

Five basic milieus in the 'adventure society'
Source: Schulze 1993

Quality milieu	Harmony milieu	Integration milieu	Self realization milieu	Entertainment milieu
typical of over 40 year olds with higher education and good job	typical of over 40 year olds with lower level of education and dependent job	petit bourgeois, middle aged and older people	represent changing values; mainly younger and middle aged people with higher education	mainly 40 year olds with lower education or insecure jobs (blue collar workers, young people)
achievement, order and perfection	family oriented, petit bourgeois	strive for harmony in clubs	may take part in protest movements	seek action – and satisfaction
interested in fine arts and high culture	attend funfairs and member of *Vereine* (clubs)	prefer to watch TV; enjoy light as well as classical music	new culture scene (for example, multicultural bars and inns)	often go to fan clubs, disco clubs, motorcycle clubs etc.
enjoy antiques, motorcycle clubs, etc.	plush and comfortable style	country style, orderly, antique furniture	partly counter culture, parsimonious, intellectual, neglect day to day things	stereos and videos permanently on

The unification of Germany brought together two very different social systems.

How different groups see themselves in the status pyramid east Germany

Source: *Datenreport* 1994

6%

77%

17%
self employed

Even in 1994 people in the eastern Länder found themselves at the bottom of the social hierarchy.

4%

87%

9%
senior white collar workers

13%

87%

civil servants

The political system of East Germany was totally restructured, but its systems of education and training were similar to those in West Germany. This is why three quarters of the workforce has remained in similar jobs to the ones they had before unification.

8%

92%
semi/ unskilled workers

6%

94%
skilled workers

2%

59%

39%
middle rank white collar workers

east

How people perceive their own social position, east Germany *1994*

Source: Noll 1995

○ upper class and upper middle class 👤

○ middle class 👤

○ lower and working class 👤

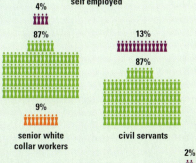

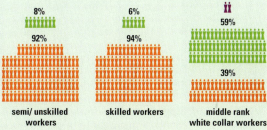

Opportunities for higher school and education certificates for children and young people in Germany Source: Geißler 1996

Opportunities	Education/Job of head of household
very good	self employed academics civil servants/white collar workers with Abitur (leaving certificate)
good	civil servants/white collar workers with intermediate leaving certificate
fair	non academic self employed (excluding farmers); civil servants/white collar workers with intermediate final exam
disadvantaged	independent farmers skilled blue collar workers
very disadvantaged	unskilled blue collar workers

Professional mobility from the GDR to east Germany *1989-93*
Share of people who have remained in the same job position as in 1989
percentages

Source: Diewald/Sørensen 1996

29

Bernhard Schäfers *The State of Germany Atlas* Copyright © Myriad Editions Limited

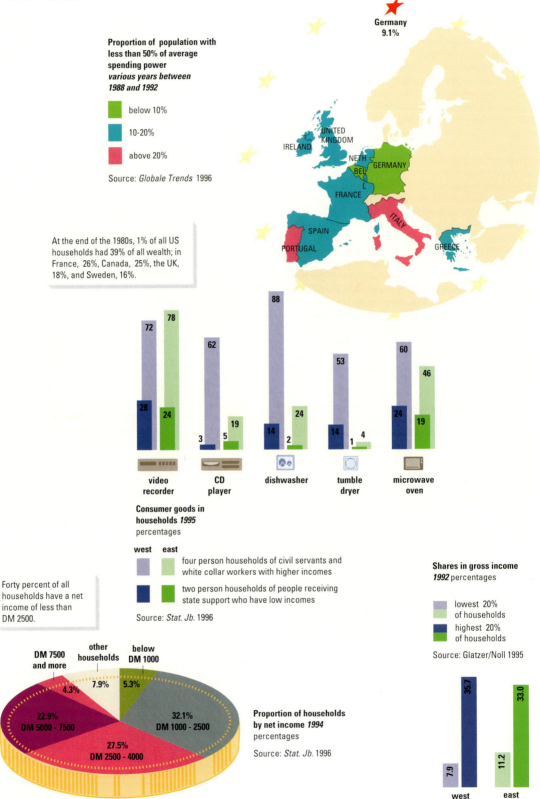

Proportion of population with less than 50% of average spending power
various years between 1988 and 1992

- below 10%
- 10-20%
- above 20%

Source: *Globale Trends* 1996

Germany
9.1%

At the end of the 1980s, 1% of all US households had 39% of all wealth; in France, 26%, Canada, 25%, the UK, 18%, and Sweden, 16%.

UNITED KINGDOM
IRELAND
NETH
BEL
L
GERMANY
FRANCE
SPAIN
ITALY
PORTUGAL
GREECE

video recorder: 72, 78, 28, 24
CD player: 62, 19, 3, 5
dishwasher: 88, 24, 14, 2
tumble dryer: 53, 4, 14, 1
microwave oven: 60, 46, 24, 19

Consumer goods in households *1995*
percentages

west   east

four person households of civil servants and white collar workers with higher incomes

two person households of people receiving state support who have low incomes

Source: *Stat. Jb.* 1996

Forty percent of all households have a net income of less than DM 2500.

DM 7500 and more — 4.3%
other households — 7.9%
below DM 1000 — 5.3%
DM 5000 - 7500 — 22.9%
DM 1000 - 2500 — 32.1%
DM 2500 - 4000 — 27.5%

Proportion of households by net income *1994*
percentages

Source: *Stat. Jb.* 1996

Shares in gross income *1992* percentages

- lowest 20% of households
- highest 20% of households

Source: Glatzer/Noll 1995

west: 7.9, 35.7
east: 11.2, 33.0

Since the mid 1970s, poverty has been increasing in Germany.

Spending on income support in Hamburg
1970-93

2120
1700
540
137
1970 1980 1990 1993

The city of Hamburg has the highest number of poor people compared with rich.

In 1995, 3.5 million households, or 10 million people, lived in poverty.

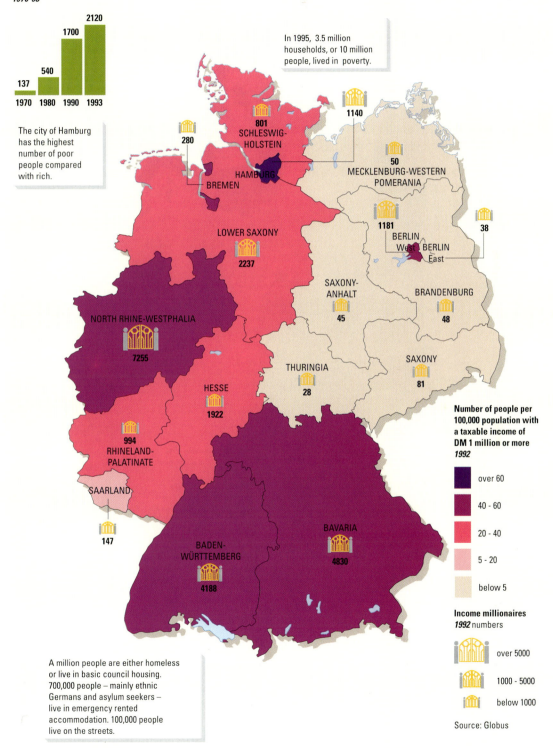

SCHLESWIG-HOLSTEIN 801

280

1140

HAMBURG

BREMEN

50
MECKLENBURG-WESTERN POMERANIA

LOWER SAXONY 2237

1181
BERLIN
West BERLIN East

38

NORTH RHINE-WESTPHALIA 7255

SAXONY-ANHALT 45

BRANDENBURG 48

HESSE 1922

THURINGIA 28

SAXONY 81

994
RHINELAND-PALATINATE

SAARLAND

147

BADEN-WÜRTTEMBERG 4188

BAVARIA 4830

Number of people per 100,000 population with a taxable income of DM 1 million or more
1992

- over 60
- 40 - 60
- 20 - 40
- 5 - 20
- below 5

Income millionaires
1992 numbers

- over 5000
- 1000 - 5000
- below 1000

Source: Globus

A million people are either homeless or live in basic council housing. 700,000 people – mainly ethnic Germans and asylum seekers – live in emergency rented accommodation. 100,000 people live on the streets.

Bernhard Schäfers *The State of Germany Atlas* Copyright © Myriad Editions Limited

Student numbers
1975 and 1992 millions

- Japan
- USA
- France
- UK
- Italy
- Germany

Source: Bundesmin. für Bildung

1975
- 1.8
- 7.2
- 0.8
- 0.3
- 1
- 1.2

1992
- 2.9
- 14.4
- 2.0
- 1.4
- 1.6
- 1.9

Germany
2.6%

IRELAND
UNITED KINGDOM
DENMARK
NETH
BEL
GERMANY
L
FRANCE
SPAIN
PORTUGAL
ITALY
GREECE

In 1995, a fifth of all young people became unemployed after completing their vocational training; in east Germany, as many as a third.

SCHLESWIG-HOLSTEIN
HAMBURG
BREMEN
MECKLENBURG-WESTERN POMERANIA
LOWER SAXONY
BRANDENBURG
BERLIN
SAXONY-ANHALT
NORTH RHINE-WESTPHALIA
HESSE
THURINGIA
SAXONY
RHINELAND-PALATINATE
SAARLAND
BADEN-WÜRTTEMBERG
BAVARIA

Students in tertiary education in the EU, *1992* percentages of population

- 3% and more
- 2 - 2.9%
- below 2%

Source: Bundesmin. für Bildung

Research spending *1995*
DM per head of population

- DM 600 and more
- 500 - 600
- 400 - 500
- 300 - 400
- below DM 300

Highest: Berlin DM 945

Source: Globus

Only 15% of businesses with below 4 employees train apprentices, compared with 37% of those with 4 to 50 employees, 60% with 50 to 500, and 82% with more than 500.

786,000
trade and industry

567,700
crafts

156,900
independent professionals

73,300
public service

29,700
agri-culture

12,600
domestic science

Apprentices by sector *1994*
numbers

5000 apprentices

Source: Bundesmin. für Bildung

As work becomes more dependent upon technology, there are growing pressures to improve education and training.

Germany's university students are the oldest in Europe. Their average age when they first go to university is nearly 22. When they reach their final year, they are 28.

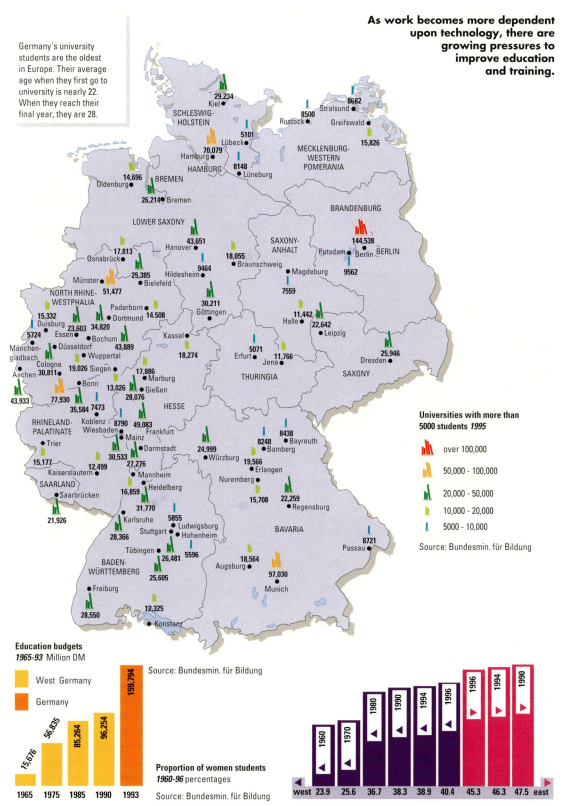

29,234 Kiel
SCHLESWIG-HOLSTEIN
8682 Stralsund
8500 Rostock
Greifswald
5101 Lübeck
15,826
70,079 Hamburg
HAMBURG
8148 Lüneburg
14,696 Oldenburg
BREMEN
MECKLENBURG-WESTERN POMERANIA
26,214 Bremen
LOWER SAXONY
BRANDENBURG
43,651 Hanover
SAXONY-ANHALT
144,538 Potsdam Berlin BERLIN
17,813 Osnabrück
18,055 Braunschweig
9562
Münster
9464 Hildesheim
Magdeburg
25,385 Bielefeld
NORTH RHINE-WESTPHALIA 51,477
30,211 Göttingen
7559
15,332 Duisburg
Paderborn 14.508 Dortmund
11,442 Halle
22,642 Leipzig
5724 Essen
23,603 34,820 Bochum
Kassel
Mönchen-gladbach
43,889 Wuppertal
18,274
5071 Erfurt
11,766 Jena
25,946 Dresden
Cologne 19,026 Siegen
17,886 Marburg
THURINGIA
SAXONY
Aachen 30,811 Bonn
13,026 Gießen
43,933 77,930
28,076
35,584 7473 Koblenz 8790 49,083
HESSE
RHINELAND-PALATINATE Wiesbaden Mainz Frankfurt
Trier
24,999 Würzburg
8438 Bayreuth
8248 Bamberg
15,177 Kaiserslautern
12,499 30,533 27,276 Darmstadt
Mannheim
19,566 Erlangen
Nuremberg
16,859 Heidelberg
15,708
22,259 Regensburg
21,926
SAARLAND Saarbrücken
31,770 Karlsruhe
5855 Ludwigsburg
Stuttgart Hohenheim
BAVARIA
8721 Passau
28,366 Tübingen
26,481 5596
18,564 Augsburg
97,030 Munich
BADEN-WÜRTTEMBERG
25,605
Freiburg
12,325 Konstanz
28,550

Universities with more than 5000 students *1995*

- over 100,000
- 50,000 - 100,000
- 20,000 - 50,000
- 10,000 - 20,000
- 5000 - 10,000

Source: Bundesmin. für Bildung

Education budgets
1965-93 Million DM

Source: Bundesmin. für Bildung

West Germany
Germany

1965	1975	1985	1990	1993
15,676	56,835	85,264	96,254	159,794

Proportion of women students
1960-96 percentages

Source: Bundesmin. für Bildung

west	1960	1970	1980	1990	1994	1996	1996	1994	1990	east
23.9	25.6	36.7	38.3	38.9	40.4	45.3	46.3	47.5		

Religion of father of live births within marriage *1994* numbers
Sources: *Stat. Jb.* 1996

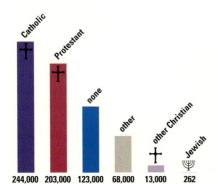

Catholic	Protestant	none	other	other Christian	Jewish
244,000	203,000	123,000	68,000	13,000	262

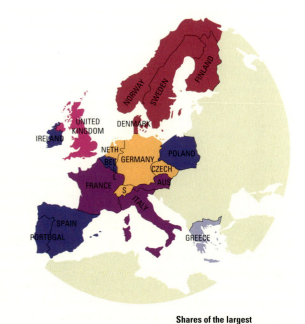

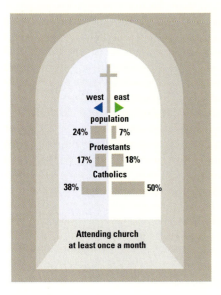

west ◀ east ▶
population
24% — 7%
Protestants
17% — 18%
Catholics
38% — 50%

Attending church at least once a month

Church attendance *1993*
percentages
Source: *Datenreport* 1994

Shares of the largest religious group in the population *1993*
percentages

Catholics

 over 90%

 75 - 90%

Protestants

over 75%

50 - 75%

98% Greek Orthodox

no religious community over 50%

Sources: *Stat. Jb. Ausland* 1995;
Fischer Weltalmanach '96

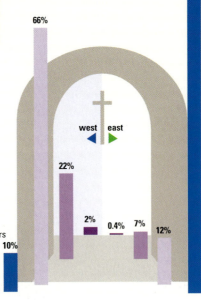

80%

66%

west ◀ east ▶

22%

2%   0.4%   7%   12%

10%

Young people and the church (aged 13 to 29) *1992* percentages

- ▮ no connection
- ▮ marginal members
- ▮ churchgoers
- ▮ core members

Source: *Jugend '92*

One in two people in west Germany, but only one in five in east Germany say that religious belief is important to their wellbeing.

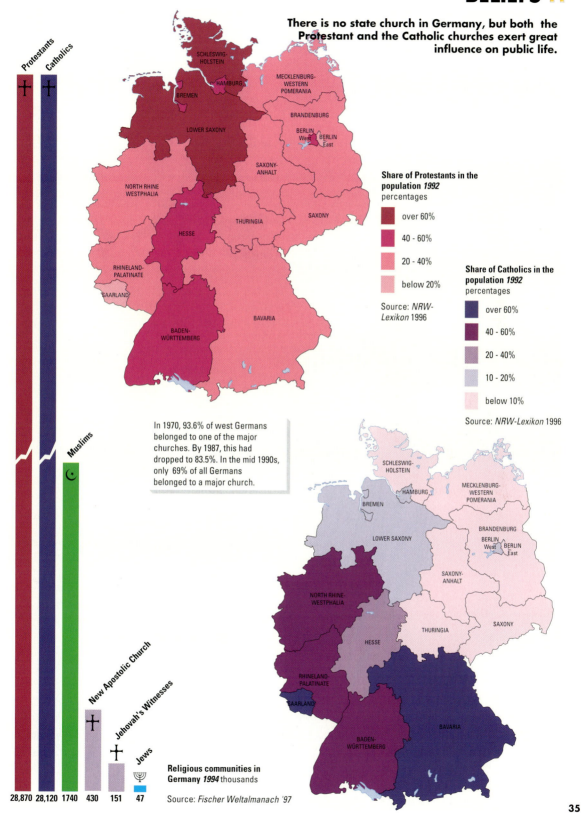

There is no state church in Germany, but both the Protestant and the Catholic churches exert great influence on public life.

Protestants

Catholics

Muslims

New Apostolic Church

Jehovah's Witnesses

Jews

Share of Protestants in the population *1992*
percentages

- over 60%
- 40 - 60%
- 20 - 40%
- below 20%

Source: *NRW-Lexikon* 1996

Share of Catholics in the population *1992*
percentages

- over 60%
- 40 - 60%
- 20 - 40%
- 10 - 20%
- below 10%

Source: *NRW-Lexikon* 1996

In 1970, 93.6% of west Germans belonged to one of the major churches. By 1987, this had dropped to 83.5%. In the mid 1990s, only 69% of all Germans belonged to a major church.

Religious communities in Germany *1994* thousands

| 28,870 | 28,120 | 1740 | 430 | 151 | 47 |

Source: *Fischer Weltalmanach '97*

35

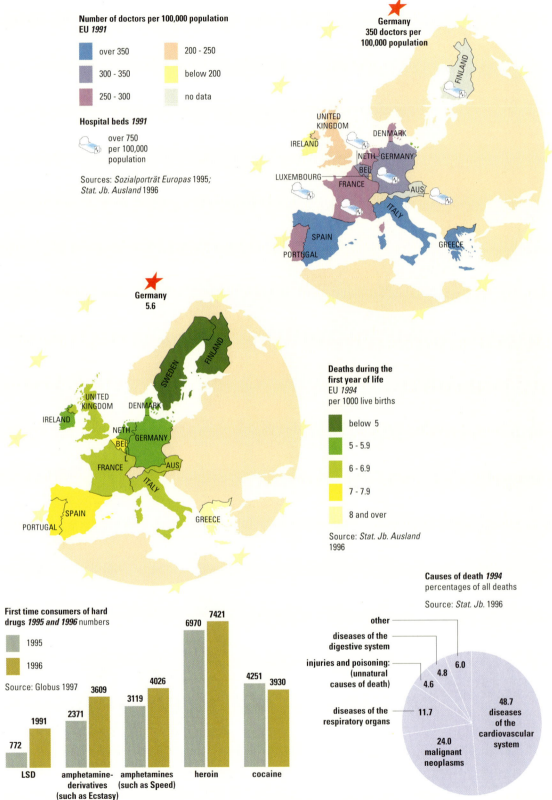

Number of doctors per 100,000 population
EU *1991*

- over 350
- 300 - 350
- 250 - 300
- 200 - 250
- below 200
- no data

Hospital beds *1991*

over 750
per 100,000
population

Sources: *Sozialporträt Europas* 1995;
Stat. Jb. Ausland 1996

Germany
350 doctors per
100,000 population

FINLAND

UNITED
KINGDOM
IRELAND
DENMARK
NETH. GERMANY
BEL
LUXEMBOURG
FRANCE
AUS
ITALY
SPAIN
GREECE
PORTUGAL

Germany
5.6

SWEDEN
FINLAND
UNITED
KINGDOM
DENMARK
IRELAND
NETH
BEL
GERMANY
FRANCE
AUS
ITALY
SPAIN
GREECE
PORTUGAL

Deaths during the
first year of life
EU *1994*
per 1000 live births

- below 5
- 5 - 5.9
- 6 - 6.9
- 7 - 7.9
- 8 and over

Source: *Stat. Jb. Ausland*
1996

First time consumers of hard
drugs *1995 and 1996* numbers

- 1995
- 1996

Source: Globus 1997

	LSD	amphetamine-derivatives (such as Ecstasy)	amphetamines (such as Speed)	heroin	cocaine
1995	772	2371	3119	6970	4251
1996	1991	3609	4026	7421	3930

Causes of death *1994*
percentages of all deaths

Source: *Stat. Jb.* 1996

- other — 6.0
- diseases of the digestive system — 4.8
- injuries and poisoning: (unnatural causes of death) — 4.6
- diseases of the respiratory organs — 11.7
- 48.7 diseases of the cardiovascular system
- 24.0 malignant neoplasms

The health system is rated highly but Germans are having to spend more on their rising health needs from their own pockets.

Health is dear to the hearts of Germans. Ten percent of gross domestic product (GDP) is spent on health and 7 percent of the workforce in Germany is employed in health care.

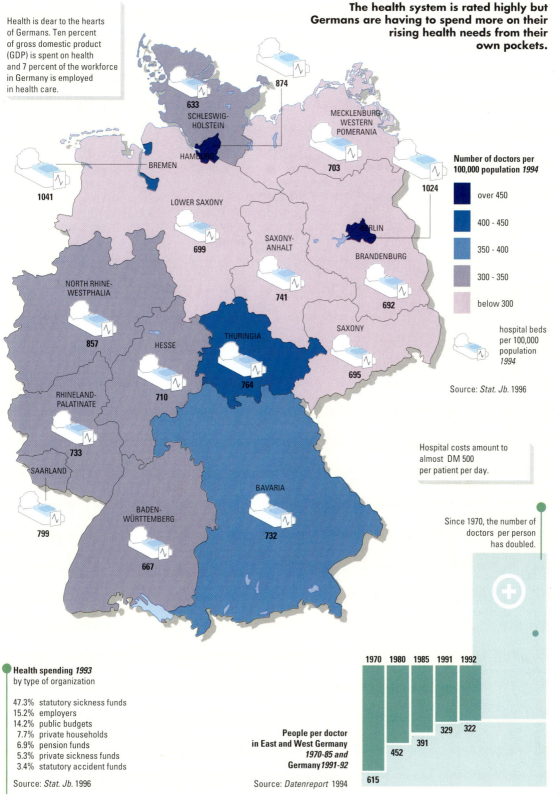

874

633
SCHLESWIG-HOLSTEIN

MECKLENBURG-WESTERN POMERANIA

703

HAMBURG

BREMEN

1041

1024

LOWER SAXONY

BERLIN

SAXONY-ANHALT

BRANDENBURG

699

741

692

NORTH RHINE-WESTPHALIA

857

HESSE

THURINGIA

SAXONY

710

764

695

RHINELAND-PALATINATE

733

SAARLAND

BAVARIA

799

BADEN-WÜRTTEMBERG

732

667

Number of doctors per 100,000 population *1994*

- over 450
- 400 - 450
- 350 - 400
- 300 - 350
- below 300

hospital beds per 100,000 population *1994*

Source: *Stat. Jb.* 1996

Hospital costs amount to almost DM 500 per patient per day.

Since 1970, the number of doctors per person has doubled.

1970	1980	1985	1991	1992
			329	322
		391		
	452			
615				

People per doctor in East and West Germany *1970-85 and* **Germany** *1991-92*

Source: *Datenreport* 1994

Health spending *1993* by type of organization

47.3% statutory sickness funds
15.2% employers
14.2% public budgets
7.7% private households
6.9% pension funds
5.3% private sickness funds
3.4% statutory accident funds

Source: *Stat. Jb.* 1996

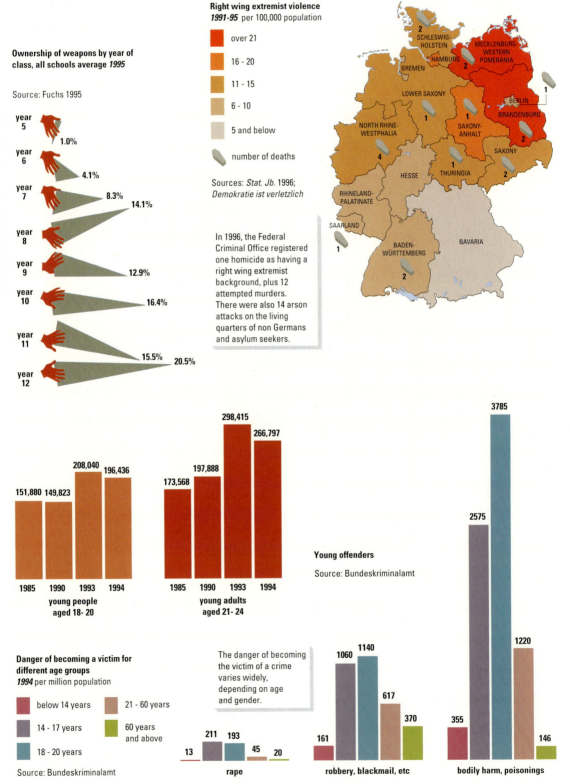

Bernhard Schäfers *The State of Germany Atlas* Copyright © Myriad Editions Limited

Ownership of weapons by year of class, all schools average *1995*

Source: Fuchs 1995

year 5 — 1.0%
year 6 — 4.1%
year 7 — 8.3%
— 14.1%
year 8
year 9 — 12.9%
year 10 — 16.4%
year 11
year 12 — 15.5% — 20.5%

Right wing extremist violence
1991-95 per 100,000 population

- over 21
- 16 - 20
- 11 - 15
- 6 - 10
- 5 and below
- number of deaths

Sources: *Stat. Jb.* 1996;
Demokratie ist verletzlich

In 1996, the Federal Criminal Office registered one homicide as having a right wing extremist background, plus 12 attempted murders. There were also 14 arson attacks on the living quarters of non Germans and asylum seekers.

SCHLESWIG-HOLSTEIN — 2
HAMBURG
MECKLENBURG WESTERN POMERANIA — 2
BREMEN
LOWER SAXONY — 1
BERLIN — 1
NORTH RHINE-WESTPHALIA — 4
BRANDENBURG
SAXONY-ANHALT — 1 — 2
HESSE
THURINGIA — 1
SAXONY — 2
RHINELAND-PALATINATE
SAARLAND — 1
BADEN-WÜRTTEMBERG — 2
BAVARIA

young people aged 18- 20
1985 — 151,880
1990 — 149,823
1993 — 208,040
1994 — 196,436

young adults aged 21- 24
1985 — 173,568
1990 — 197,888
1993 — 298,415
1994 — 266,797

Young offenders

Source: Bundeskriminalamt

Danger of becoming a victim for different age groups
1994 per million population

- below 14 years
- 14 - 17 years
- 18 - 20 years
- 21 - 60 years
- 60 years and above

Source: Bundeskriminalamt

The danger of becoming the victim of a crime varies widely, depending on age and gender.

rape
13
211
193
45
20

robbery, blackmail, etc
161
1060
1140
617
370

bodily harm, poisonings
355
2575
3785
1220
146

Proportion of population worried about crime *1994*

percentages

west ◀		east ▶
55%	total	72%
46%	18 - 34 yrs	60%
57%	35 - 59 yrs	75%
65%	over 60 yrs	83%

Source: *Datenreport* 1994

Criminals are more likely to be men than women, more likely to be young than old, and are more likely to live in cities.

In 1992, 1570 (4%) of all convicted prisoners were female.

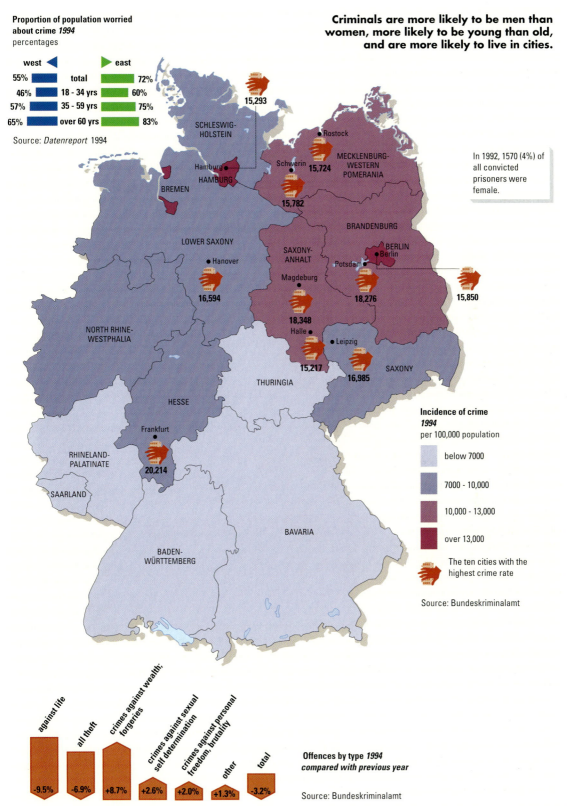

SCHLESWIG-HOLSTEIN

15,293

● Rostock

Schwerin ● MECKLENBURG-WESTERN POMERANIA
15,724

Hamburg ●
HAMBURG
15,782

BREMEN

BRANDENBURG

LOWER SAXONY

● Hanover
16,594

SAXONY-ANHALT

Magdeburg ●

Potsdam ●

BERLIN
● Berlin
18,276

15,850

NORTH RHINE-WESTPHALIA

18,348

Halle ●
15,217

● Leipzig
16,985

SAXONY

THURINGIA

HESSE

Frankfurt ●
20,214

RHINELAND-PALATINATE

SAARLAND

BAVARIA

BADEN-WÜRTTEMBERG

Incidence of crime *1994*
per 100,000 population

- below 7000
- 7000 - 10,000
- 10,000 - 13,000
- over 13,000

The ten cities with the highest crime rate

Source: Bundeskriminalamt

against life	all theft	crimes against wealth; forgeries	crimes against sexual self determination	crimes against personal freedom, brutality	other	total
-9.5%	-6.9%	+8.7%	+2.6%	+2.0%	+1.3%	-3.2%

Offences by type *1994*
compared with previous year

Source: Bundeskriminalamt

PCs per 100 population *end 1995*

Sources: *Info 2000* 1996

USA 39
Switzerland 33
Norway 30
Denmark 27
Sweden 26
Netherlands 22
UK 20
Germany 19
Finland 18
Belgium 16
France 14
Japan 14
Austria 14
Italy 10
Spain 9

Cable connections in western Europe *1993* percentages

- over 90%
- 65 - 90%
- 40 - 65%
- 15 - 40%
- below 15%

Source: Kleinsteuber/Rossmann 1994

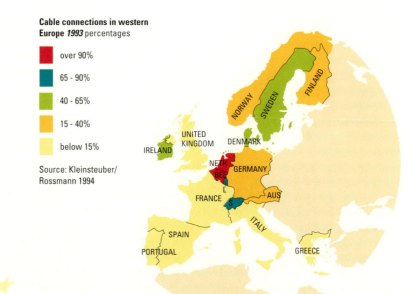

Daily newspapers
1991 copies per 1000 population

- over 350
- 300 - 350
- 150 - 200
- 100 - 150
- below 100

over 100 different daily newspapers

Source: Kleinsteuber/Rossmann 1994

In 1993, a third of all large cities had a local daily newspaper, and almost half had two or more local papers produced by different publishers. There were 1601 daily newspapers altogether and 25.3 million copies were printed, of which 6.2 million were tabloids.

Some media are evenly distributed, east and west. This not yet true of those media requiring their own infrastructure, such as cable.

Interactive media by household
1995 and forecast for 2000

on line-services:
1995: 1.4 million
2000: 2.8 million

interactive TV:
1995: 0.1 million
2000: 1.9 million

CD-ROM drives:
1995: 2 million
2000: 15.8 million

Source: Jäschke-Optimum Media

Share of middle income, four person households with PCs *1986-95*
percentages

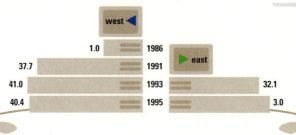

	west		east
1986	1.0		
1991	37.7		
1993	41.0		32.1
1995	40.4		3.0

Sources: *Stat. Jb.* 1989, 1992, 1996

In Germany as elsewhere, the expansion of electronic media marks the beginning of an information society.

In April 1996, 24.4 million households (two thirds of the total) had a cable connection; 16 million households actually used it.

In east Germany, private radio and television channels are more popular than public ones.

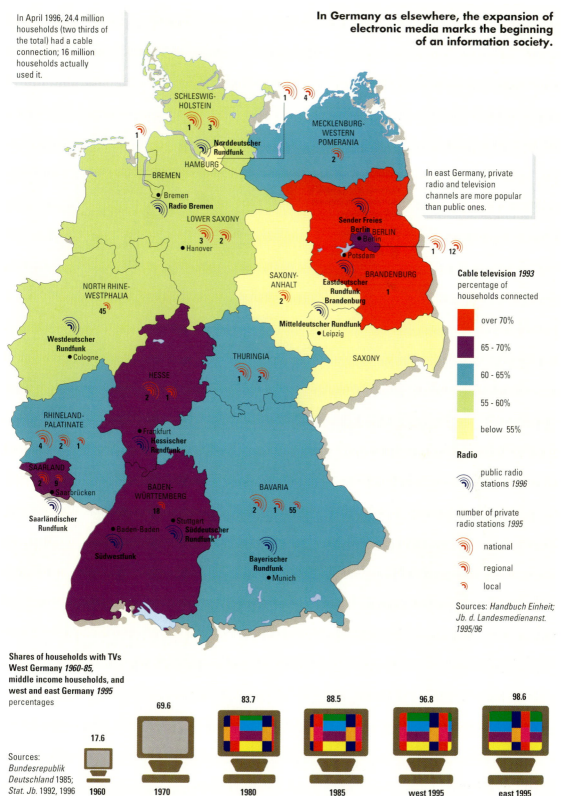

SCHLESWIG-HOLSTEIN

1   4

1   3

1

Norddeutscher Rundfunk

HAMBURG

MECKLENBURG-WESTERN POMERANIA

2

BREMEN

• Bremen   Radio Bremen

LOWER SAXONY

3   2
• Hanover

Sender Freies Berlin BERLIN
• Berlin
• Potsdam

1   12

BRANDENBURG

Eastdeutscher Rundfunk Brandenburg

1

NORTH RHINE-WESTPHALIA

45

Westdeutscher Rundfunk
• Cologne

SAXONY-ANHALT

2

Mitteldeutscher Rundfunk
• Leipzig

THURINGIA

1   2

SAXONY

HESSE

2   1

RHINELAND-PALATINATE

4   2   1

• Frankfurt
Hessischer Rundfunk

SAARLAND

2   9
• Saarbrücken

Saarländischer Rundfunk

BADEN-WÜRTTEMBERG

18

• Stuttgart
Süddeutscher Rundfunk

• Baden-Baden

Südwestfunk

BAVARIA

2   1   55

Bayerischer Rundfunk
• Munich

Cable television *1993*
percentage of households connected

- over 70%
- 65 - 70%
- 60 - 65%
- 55 - 60%
- below 55%

Radio

public radio stations *1996*

number of private radio stations *1995*

national

regional

local

Sources: *Handbuch Einheit; Jb. d. Landesmedienanst. 1995/96*

Shares of households with TVs West Germany *1960-85*, middle income households, and west and east Germany *1995* percentages

Sources: *Bundesrepublik Deutschland* 1985; *Stat. Jb.* 1992, 1996

Year	Percentage
1960	17.6
1970	69.6
1980	83.7
1985	88.5
west 1995	96.8
east 1995	98.6

Bernhard Schäfers *The State of Germany Atlas* Copyright © Myriad Editions Limited

SOCIETY

The Germans are the world champions of travel.
In 1996, the World Tourism Organisation counted 75 million arrivals by German travellers. Worldwide, the number of tourist arrivals was 593 million.

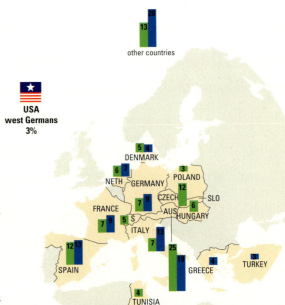

other countries

USA
west Germans
3%

DENMARK
NETH
GERMANY
POLAND
CZECH
SLO
FRANCE
AUS
HUNGARY
S
ITALY
SPAIN
GREECE
TURKEY
TUNISIA

Preferred foreign holiday destinations of Germans
1992 percentages

■ east Germans
■ west Germans

Source: *Datenreport* 1994

jury members
80,000

active voluntary workers in the Deutscher Naturschutzring
175,000

Members of the Deutscher Gewerkschaftsbund as honorary works council members for social affairs
220,000

Entrepreneurs or business representatives in the chambers of industry and commerce
250,000

Voluntary work in denominational and non denominational youth associations
800,000

Voluntary school governors
1 million

Voluntary work in the Arbeiterwohlfahrt, Deutscher Caritasverband, Deutscher Paritätischer Wohlfahrtsverband, Deutsches Rotes Kreuz, Diakonisches Werk der Evangelischen Kirche; help in emergencies
1.5 - 1.7 million

2.5 million honorary members are active in the 85,519 sports clubs.

Total number of museums in Germany: 3615

ethnic and local heritage 1745
art galleries 383
castles and palaces 182
natural history 175
science and technology 355
history and archaeology 204
other 571

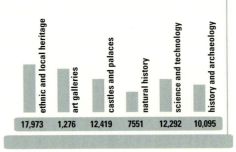

ethnic and local heritage	art galleries	castles and palaces	natural history	science and technology	history and archaeology
17,973	1,276	12,419	7551	12,292	10,095

Museums *1992*
thousands of visitors

Source: *Datenreport* 1994

Voluntary activities

Source: Bundestagsdrucksache

Time available for recreation and leisure varies widely by gender and age, occupation and income.

Not everyone in Germany lives in a 'leisure paradise'. In 1993, 73% of people in fulltime work in east Germany had 'little' or 'very little' free time, compared with 46% in the west. Men have more free time than women.

Two million people are employed in tourism and leisure and there are 75,000 apprentices in the industry.

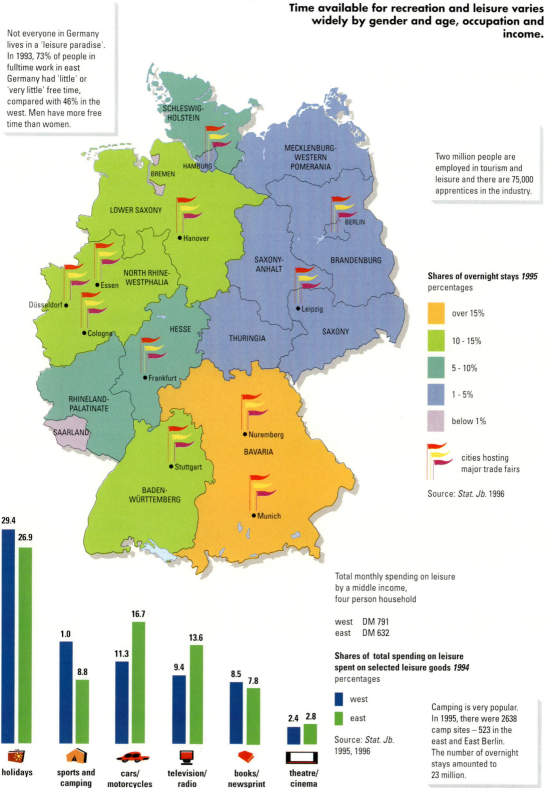

Shares of overnight stays *1995*
percentages

- over 15%
- 10 - 15%
- 5 - 10%
- 1 - 5%
- below 1%

cities hosting major trade fairs

Source: *Stat. Jb.* 1996

Total monthly spending on leisure by a middle income, four person household

west   DM 791
east   DM 632

Shares of total spending on leisure spent on selected leisure goods *1994*
percentages

- west
- east

Source: *Stat. Jb.* 1995, 1996

Camping is very popular. In 1995, there were 2638 camp sites – 523 in the east and East Berlin. The number of overnight stays amounted to 23 million.

holidays — 29.4 / 26.9
sports and camping — 1.0 / 8.8
cars/motorcycles — 11.3 / 16.7
television/radio — 9.4 / 13.6
books/newsprint — 8.5 / 7.8
theatre/cinema — 2.4 / 2.8

In small communities, active club membership provides a way into social networks. In larger cities, this can be achieved by supporting a football team, a successful sports club, or local athletes.

Club activities in a small municipality

Ebersteinburg
1996: population 1245

Fidelitas choir, founded in 1876:
280 members, 43 actively singing

Sports club of Ebersteinburg, founded in 1906: 490 members, 300 active in gymnastics, children's gymnastics, handball, tennis, skiing, combat sports

Harmonica club of Ebersteinburg:
190 members, 12 active

fruit growing and horticultural club: 70 members

Source: Schäfers

4 km from Baden-Baden and part of its urban district administration ● Ebersteinburg

Shares of population active at least in one club *1993*
percentages

west ◄		► east
55	**men**	33
39	**women**	21
47	**total**	26

Source: *Datenreport* 1994

Club members (over 14 years old) *1993* million

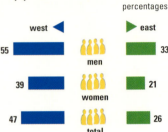

west ◄		► east
1.0	**young farmers; women's clubs**	0.1
1.0	**citizens' clubs; local heritage clubs**	0.3
1.0	**allotment clubs**	1.3
1.5	**protection of animals and nature**	0.1
2.0	**hiking clubs**	0.1
2.5	**choirs**	0.4
2.5	**rifle associations**	0.1
4.0	**church clubs**	1.1
5.4	**bowling clubs**	0.3
1.,9	**sports clubs**	1.7

Markedly more people belong to allotment clubs in the east than do so in the west..

Exploring the Alps is also a popular activity for clubs. In 1995, the Deutsche Alpenverein had 581, 000 members and kept 305 mountain cabins..

Source: *Harenberg Lexikon* 1996

Map

SCHLESWIG-HOLSTEIN
HAMBURG
MECKLENBURG-WESTERN POMERANIA
BREMEN and LOWER SAXONY
BRANDENBURG
BERLIN
NORTH RHINE-WESTPHALIA
SAXONY-ANHALT
HESSE
THURINGIA
SAXONY
RHINELAND-PALATINATE
SAARLAND
BADEN-WÜRTTEMBERG
BAVARIA

Number of choirs

- over 4000
- 3000 - 4000
- 2000 - 3000
- 1000 - 2000
- below 1000

Member choirs within regional associations

- over 1000
- 500 - 1000
- below 500

Source: *Stat. Jb.* 1996

The Germans are club enthusiasts. Most Germans belong to at least one club or welfare organization.

German sports federation *1995*
members per 100 population

- over 40
- 30 - 39
- 20 - 29
- 10 - 20
- below 10

Numbers of sports clubs *1995*

- over 10,000
- 7500 - 10,000
- 5000 - 7500
- 2500 - 5000
- below 2500

Source: *Stat. Jb.* 1996

Headquarters of umbrella welfare and charity organizations *1997*

Arbeiterwohlfahrt German Red Cross

Deutscher Paritätischer Wohlfahrtsverband Central welfare office of Jews in Germany

Diakonisches Werk of the Protestant church

Deutscher Caritasverband

Bonn
Frankfurt
Stuttgart
Freiburg

Umbrella organizations in voluntary welfare work

- institutions
- employees (fulltime and parttime)

Source: *Taschenb. d. öff. Lebens Deutschland* 1996/97

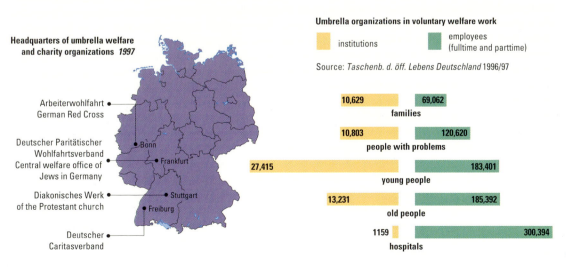

	institutions	employees
families	10,629	69,062
people with problems	10,803	120,620
young people	27,415	183,401
old people	13,231	185,392
hospitals	1159	300,394

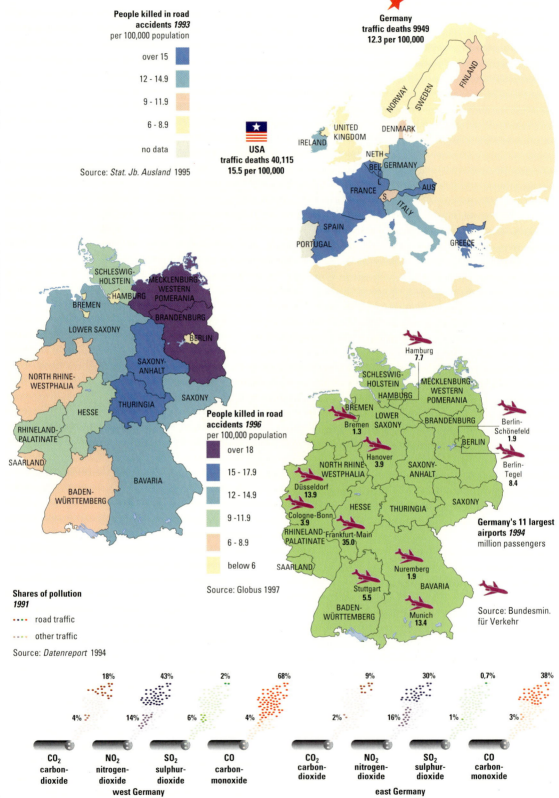

Bernhard Schäfers *The State of Germany Atlas* Copyright © Myriad Editions Limited

People killed in road accidents *1993*
per 100,000 population

- over 15
- 12 - 14.9
- 9 - 11.9
- 6 - 8.9
- no data

Source: *Stat. Jb. Ausland* 1995

USA
traffic deaths 40,115
15.5 per 100,000

Germany
traffic deaths 9949
12.3 per 100,000

NORWAY
SWEDEN
FINLAND
UNITED KINGDOM
DENMARK
IRELAND
NETH
GERMANY
BEL
L
AUS
FRANCE
S
ITALY
SPAIN
PORTUGAL
GREECE

SCHLESWIG-HOLSTEIN
HAMBURG
BREMEN
MECKLENBURG WESTERN POMERANIA
LOWER SAXONY
BRANDENBURG
BERLIN
SAXONY-ANHALT
NORTH RHINE-WESTPHALIA
SAXONY
HESSE
THURINGIA
RHINELAND-PALATINATE
SAARLAND
BAVARIA
BADEN-WÜRTTEMBERG

People killed in road accidents *1996*
per 100,000 population

- over 18
- 15 - 17.9
- 12 - 14.9
- 9 - 11.9
- 6 - 8.9
- below 6

Source: Globus 1997

Hamburg
7.7
SCHLESWIG-HOLSTEIN
HAMBURG
MECKLENBURG WESTERN POMERANIA
BREMEN
Bremen
1.3
LOWER SAXONY
BRANDENBURG
Berlin-Schönefeld
1.9
BERLIN
Berlin-Tegel
8.4
Hanover
3.9
SAXONY-ANHALT
NORTH RHINE-WESTPHALIA
Düsseldorf
13.9
SAXONY
Cologne-Bonn
3.9
HESSE
THURINGIA
RHINELAND-PALATINATE
Frankfurt-Main
35.0
SAARLAND
Nuremberg
1.9
BAVARIA
Stuttgart
5.5
BADEN-WÜRTTEMBERG
Munich
13.4

Germany's 11 largest airports *1994*
million passengers

Source: Bundesmin. für Verkehr

Shares of pollution *1991*

- ···· road traffic
- ···· other traffic

Source: *Datenreport* 1994

west Germany

	CO_2 carbon-dioxide	NO_2 nitrogen-dioxide	SO_2 sulphur-dioxide	CO carbon-monoxide
road traffic	18%	43%	2%	68%
other traffic	4%	14%	6%	4%

east Germany

	CO_2 carbon-dioxide	NO_2 nitrogen-dioxide	SO_2 sulphur-dioxide	CO carbon-monoxide
road traffic	9%	30%	0,7%	38%
other traffic	2%	16%	1%	3%

A high density of private cars brings with it all the problems of moving – and stationary – traffic.

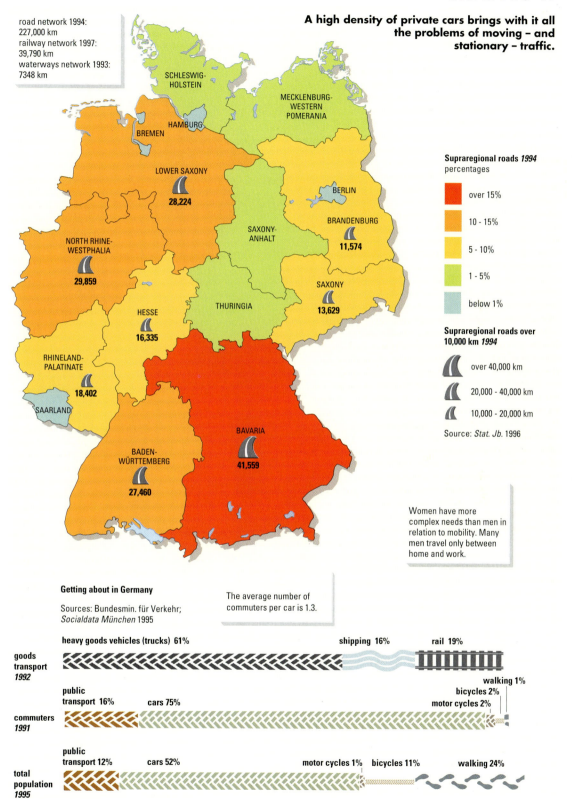

road network 1994:
227,000 km
railway network 1997:
39,790 km
waterways network 1993:
7348 km

SCHLESWIG-HOLSTEIN

MECKLENBURG-WESTERN POMERANIA

HAMBURG

BREMEN

LOWER SAXONY
28,224

BERLIN

BRANDENBURG
11,574

NORTH RHINE-WESTPHALIA
29,859

SAXONY-ANHALT

SAXONY
13,629

HESSE
16,335

THURINGIA

RHINELAND-PALATINATE
18,402

SAARLAND

BAVARIA
41,559

BADEN-WÜRTTEMBERG
27,460

Supraregional roads *1994*
percentages

- over 15%
- 10 - 15%
- 5 - 10%
- 1 - 5%
- below 1%

Supraregional roads over 10,000 km *1994*

- over 40,000 km
- 20,000 - 40,000 km
- 10,000 - 20,000 km

Source: *Stat. Jb.* 1996

Women have more complex needs than men in relation to mobility. Many men travel only between home and work.

Getting about in Germany

Sources: Bundesmin. für Verkehr; *Socialdata München* 1995

The average number of commuters per car is 1.3.

goods transport 1992
heavy goods vehicles (trucks) 61%   shipping 16%   rail 19%

commuters 1991
public transport 16%   cars 75%   walking 1%   bicycles 2%   motor cycles 2%

total population 1995
public transport 12%   cars 52%   motor cycles 1%   bicycles 11%   walking 24%

Part Three

WORK AND WELFARE

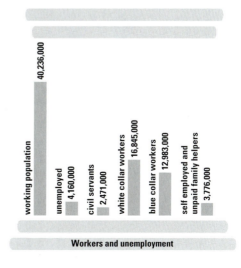

working population 40,236,000

unemployed 4,160,000

civil servants 2,471,000

white collar workers 16,845,000

blue collar workers 12,983,000

self employed and unpaid family helpers 3,776,000

Workers and unemployment

Source: Stat. Bundesamt

WORK AND WELFARE

Within the European Union, the proportion of women in paid employment is highest in Sweden (49%) and lowest in Spain (33%).

Germany
workforce 48.8%
share of women in workforce 42.0%

Japan
workforce
53.7%
share of women in workforce 40.5%

USA
workforce 51.3%
share of women in workforce 46.0%

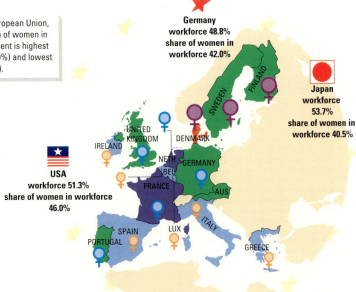

Shares of population in workforce, EU *1994*

- 52.1 - 56%
- 48.1 - 52%
- 44.1 - 48%
- 40 - 44%

Shares of women in the workforce
***1994* percentages**

- 33 - 40%
- 45.1 - 50%
- 40.1 - 45%

Source: *Stat. Jb. Ausland* 1996

Workforce with 2nd level primary school leaving certificate: west 47%, east 18%; with intermediate certificate: west 24%, east 61%.

east
work is 'very important'
82%

west
work is 'very important'
37%

Attitudes to work
Source: Mau 1996

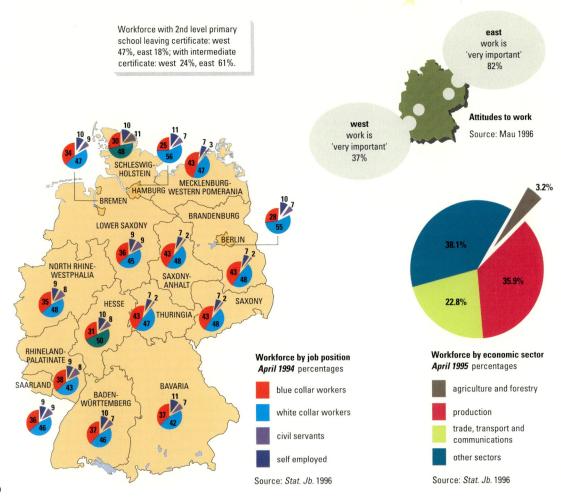

SCHLESWIG-HOLSTEIN — 10, 11, 30, 48

HAMBURG — 10, 9, 34, 47

BREMEN

MECKLENBURG-WESTERN POMERANIA — 11, 7, 25, 56 / 7, 3, 43, 47

LOWER SAXONY — 9, 9, 36, 45

BRANDENBURG — 10, 7, 28, 55

BERLIN — 7, 2, 43, 48

NORTH RHINE-WESTPHALIA — 9, 8, 35, 48

SAXONY-ANHALT — 7, 2, 43, 48

HESSE — 10, 8, 31, 50

THURINGIA — 7, 2, 43, 47

SAXONY — 7, 2, 43, 48

RHINELAND-PALATINATE — 9, 8, 38, 43

SAARLAND — 9, 9, 36, 46

BADEN-WÜRTTEMBERG — 10, 7, 37, 46

BAVARIA — 11, 7, 37, 42

Workforce by job position
April 1994 percentages

- blue collar workers
- white collar workers
- civil servants
- self employed

Source: *Stat. Jb.* 1996

Workforce by economic sector
April 1995 percentages

- 3.2% agriculture and forestry
- 35.9% production
- 22.8% trade, transport and communications
- 38.1% other sectors

Source: *Stat. Jb.* 1996

Jobs and professions tend to signify social position.

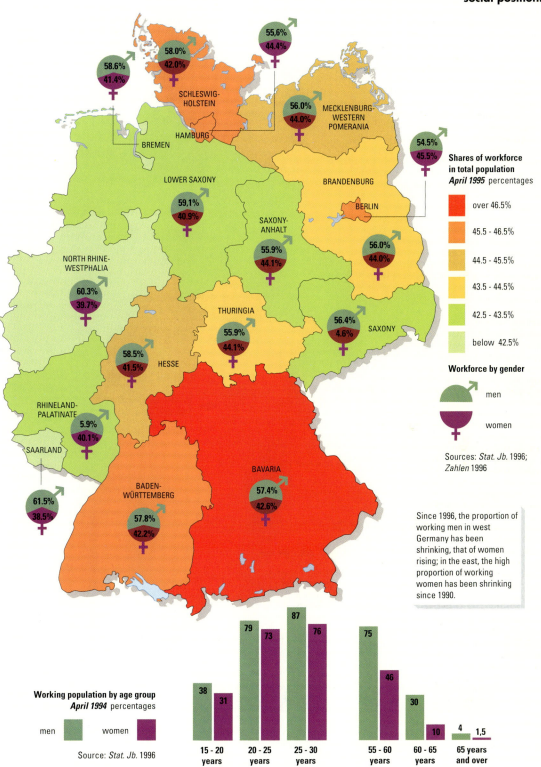

58.6%
41.4%

58.0%
42.0%

55,6%
44.4%

SCHLESWIG-HOLSTEIN

56.0%
44.0%

MECKLENBURG-WESTERN POMERANIA

HAMBURG

BREMEN

54.5%
45.5%

LOWER SAXONY

BRANDENBURG

59,1%
40.9%

BERLIN

SAXONY-ANHALT

55.9%
44.1%

56.0%
44.0%

NORTH RHINE-WESTPHALIA

60.3%
39.7%

THURINGIA

55.9%
44.1%

56.4%
4.6%

SAXONY

58.5%
41.5%

HESSE

RHINELAND-PALATINATE

5.9%
40.1%

SAARLAND

61.5%
38.5%

BADEN-WÜRTTEMBERG

57.8%
42.2%

BAVARIA

57.4%
42.6%

Shares of workforce in total population
April 1995 percentages

🟥	over 46.5%
🟧	45.5 - 46.5%
🟫	44.5 - 45.5%
🟨	43.5 - 44.5%
🟩	42.5 - 43.5%
🟢	below 42.5%

Workforce by gender

men

women

Sources: *Stat. Jb.* 1996;
Zahlen 1996

Since 1996, the proportion of working men in west Germany has been shrinking, that of women rising; in the east, the high proportion of working women has been shrinking since 1990.

Working population by age group
April 1994 percentages

men   women

Source: *Stat. Jb.* 1996

	15 - 20 years	20 - 25 years	25 - 30 years	55 - 60 years	60 - 65 years	65 years and over
men	38	79	87	75	30	4
women	31	73	76	46	10	1,5

WORK AND WELFARE

For 92% of all 12 - 24 year olds, unemployment is the biggest social problem.

Source: Shell-Jugendstudie 1997

Additional labour costs *1995*
as percentage of the net wage in industry

west Germany
total 80%
statutory 36%
locally negotiated 44%

east Germany
total 70%
statutory 36%
locally negotiated 34%

Source: *Zahlen* 1996

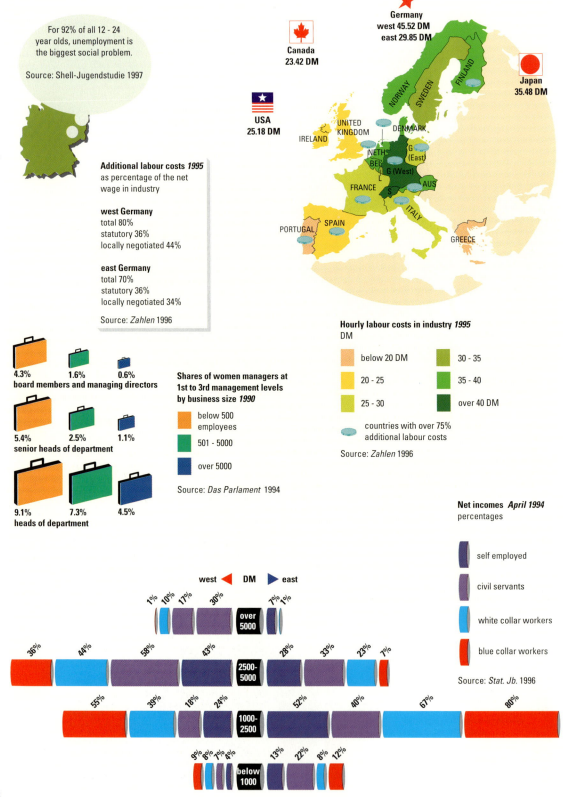

Germany
west 45.52 DM
east 29.85 DM

Canada
23.42 DM

USA
25.18 DM

Japan
35.48 DM

NORWAY
SWEDEN
FINLAND
IRELAND
UNITED KINGDOM
DENMARK
NETHS
BEL
L
G (East)
G (West)
FRANCE
S
AUS
ITALY
PORTUGAL
SPAIN
GREECE

Hourly labour costs in industry *1995*
DM

- below 20 DM
- 20 - 25
- 25 - 30
- 30 - 35
- 35 - 40
- over 40 DM

countries with over 75% additional labour costs

Source: *Zahlen* 1996

4.3%   1.6%   0.6%
board members and managing directors

5.4%   2.5%   1.1%
senior heads of department

9.1%   7.3%   4.5%
heads of department

Shares of women managers at 1st to 3rd management levels by business size *1990*

- below 500 employees
- 501 - 5000
- over 5000

Source: *Das Parlament* 1994

Net incomes *April 1994*
percentages

- self employed
- civil servants
- white collar workers
- blue collar workers

Source: *Stat. Jb.* 1996

west ◄ DM ► east

over 5000
1% 10% 17% 30%   7% 1%

2500-5000
36% 44% 58% 43%   28% 33% 23% 7%

1000-2500
55% 39% 18% 24%   52% 40% 67% 80%

below 1000
9% 8% 7% 4%   13% 22% 8% 12%

Wages and salaries reinforce social distinctions.

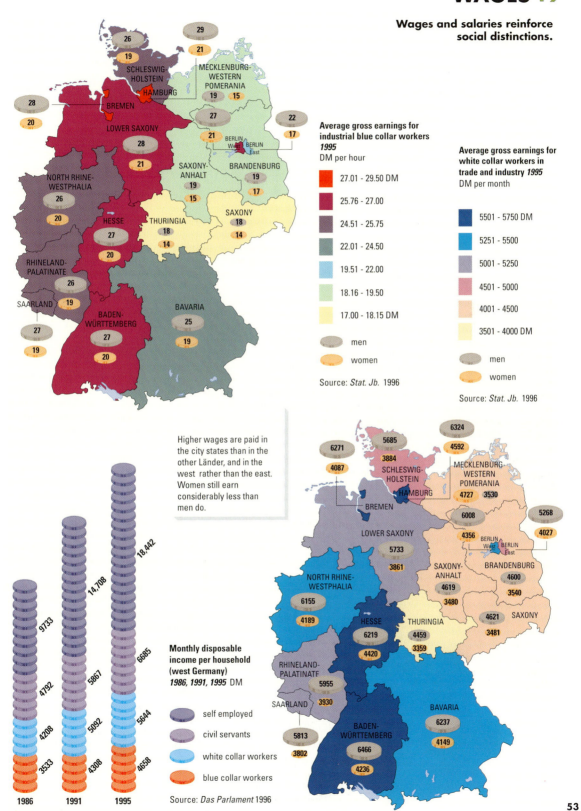

Average gross earnings for industrial blue collar workers 1995
DM per hour

- 27.01 - 29.50 DM
- 25.76 - 27.00
- 24.51 - 25.75
- 22.01 - 24.50
- 19.51 - 22.00
- 18.16 - 19.50
- 17.00 - 18.15 DM

- men
- women

Source: *Stat. Jb.* 1996

Average gross earnings for white collar workers in trade and industry 1995
DM per month

- 5501 - 5750 DM
- 5251 - 5500
- 5001 - 5250
- 4501 - 5000
- 4001 - 4500
- 3501 - 4000 DM

- men
- women

Source: *Stat. Jb.* 1996

Higher wages are paid in the city states than in the other Länder, and in the west rather than the east. Women still earn considerably less than men do.

Monthly disposable income per household (west Germany) 1986, 1991, 1995 DM

- self employed
- civil servants
- white collar workers
- blue collar workers

Source: *Das Parlament* 1996

53

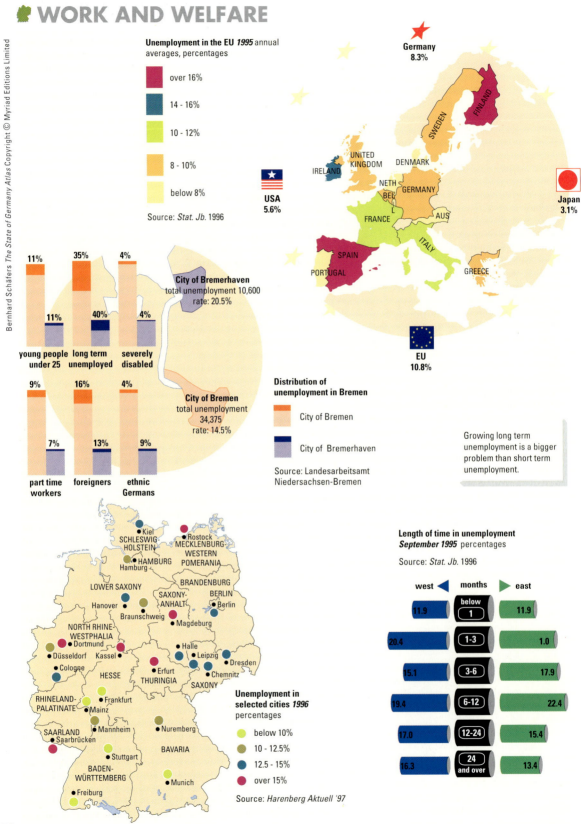

Unemployment in the EU *1995* annual averages, percentages

- over 16%
- 14 - 16%
- 10 - 12%
- 8 - 10%
- below 8%

Source: *Stat. Jb.* 1996

Germany
8.3%

USA
5.6%

Japan
3.1%

EU
10.8%

IRELAND · UNITED KINGDOM · DENMARK · NETH · BEL · L · GERMANY · FRANCE · AUS · ITALY · SWEDEN · FINLAND · SPAIN · PORTUGAL · GREECE

City of Bremerhaven
total unemployment 10,600
rate: 20.5%

City of Bremen
total unemployment
34,375
rate: 14.5%

11% · 11%
young people under 25

35% · 40%
long term unemployed

4% · 4%
severely disabled

9% · 7%
part time workers

16% · 13%
foreigners

4% · 9%
ethnic Germans

Distribution of unemployment in Bremen

- City of Bremen
- City of Bremerhaven

Source: Landesarbeitsamt Niedersachsen-Bremen

Growing long term unemployment is a bigger problem than short term unemployment.

SCHLESWIG-HOLSTEIN · Kiel
MECKLENBURG-WESTERN POMERANIA · Rostock
HAMBURG · Hamburg
LOWER SAXONY · Hanover
BRANDENBURG
SAXONY-ANHALT · Braunschweig · Magdeburg
BERLIN · Berlin
NORTH RHINE WESTPHALIA · Dortmund · Düsseldorf · Kassel · Cologne
HESSE · Halle · Leipzig · Dresden
Erfurt · Chemnitz
THURINGIA · SAXONY
RHINELAND-PALATINATE · Frankfurt · Mainz
Mannheim
SAARLAND · Saarbrücken · Nuremberg
BAVARIA
BADEN-WÜRTTEMBERG · Stuttgart · Munich
Freiburg

Unemployment in selected cities *1996* percentages

- below 10%
- 10 - 12.5%
- 12.5 - 15%
- over 15%

Source: *Harenberg Aktuell '97*

Length of time in unemployment *September 1995* percentages

Source: *Stat. Jb.* 1996

west	months	east
11.9	below 1	11.9
20.4	1-3	1.0
15.1	3-6	17.9
19.4	6-12	22.4
17.0	12-24	15.4
16.3	24 and over	13.4

As elsewhere in the European Union, unemployment has become a long term problem in Germany.

Unemployment affects young and old, academics and non academics, men and women. Increasing numbers of people are facing this experience in their lives.

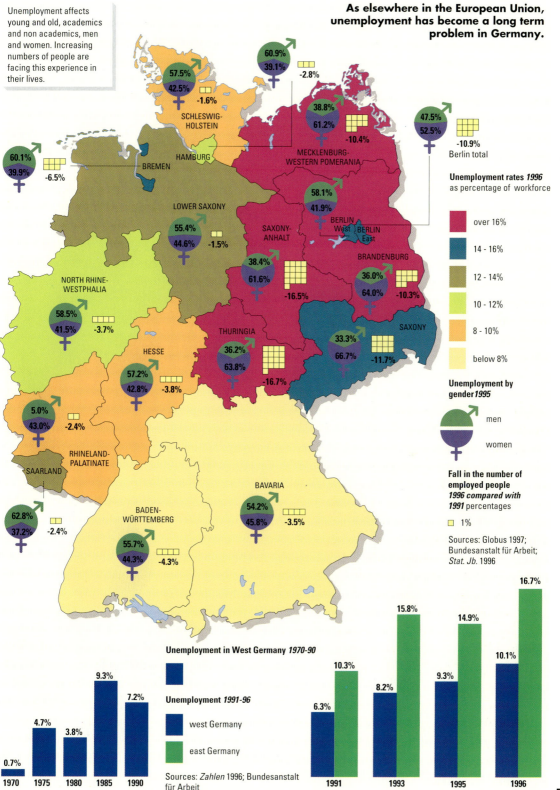

SCHLESWIG-HOLSTEIN
57.5%
42.5%
-1.6%

60.9%
39.1%
-2.8%

47.5%
52.5%
-10.9%
Berlin total

60.1%
39.9%
-6.5%

BREMEN

HAMBURG

MECKLENBURG-WESTERN POMERANIA
38.8%
61.2%
-10.4%

LOWER SAXONY
55.4%
44.6%
-1.5%

58.1%
41.9%
BERLIN West
BERLIN East

SAXONY-ANHALT
38.4%
61.6%
-16.5%

BRANDENBURG
36.0%
64.0%
-10.3%

NORTH RHINE-WESTPHALIA
58.5%
41.5%
-3.7%

HESSE
57.2%
42.8%
-3.8%

THURINGIA
36.2%
63.8%
-16.7%

SAXONY
33.3%
66.7%
-11.7%

5.0%
43.0%
-2.4%

SAARLAND
RHINELAND-PALATINATE

62.8%
37.2%
-2.4%

BADEN-WÜRTTEMBERG
55.7%
44.3%
-4.3%

BAVARIA
54.2%
45.8%
-3.5%

Unemployment rates 1996
as percentage of workforce

- over 16%
- 14 - 16%
- 12 - 14%
- 10 - 12%
- 8 - 10%
- below 8%

Unemployment by gender 1995

men

women

Fall in the number of employed people 1996 compared with 1991 percentages

☐ 1%

Sources: Globus 1997; Bundesanstalt für Arbeit; Stat. Jb. 1996

Unemployment in West Germany 1970-90

Unemployment 1991-96

west Germany

east Germany

Sources: Zahlen 1996; Bundesanstalt für Arbeit

1970	1975	1980	1985	1990
0.7%	4.7%	3.8%	9.3%	7.2%

	1991	1993	1995	1996
west Germany	6.3%	8.2%	9.3%	10.1%
east Germany	10.3%	15.8%	14.9%	16.7%

Bernhard Schäfers *The State of Germany Atlas* Copyright © Myriad Editions Limited

Shares of GDP from the informal economy:
Germany 4 - 6%
France 6 -10%
UK 8 - 12%
Italy 20 - 25%

Statutory hours worked *1995*

below 1700

1700 - 1750

1750 - 1800

over 1800

☀ 40 and more days' annual leave and bank holidays *1995*

Source: *Zahlen* 1996

★ old Länder
1602 hours; 40 days' holiday
new Länder
1705 hours; 39 days' holiday

USA
1896 hours
23 days' holiday

Japan
1832 hours
31 days' holiday

NORWAY SWEDEN FINLAND ☀
UNITED KINGDOM DENMARK
IRELAND
NETH GER E
BEL
W GER
FRANCE AUS ☀
S ITALY
SPAIN
PORTUGAL GREECE

★ **Germany**
7

Canada
137

Japan
2

USA
21

NORWAY SWEDEN FINLAND
UNITED KINGDOM DENMARK
IRELAND
NETH GERMANY
BEL
FRANCE AUS
S
SPAIN ITALY
PORTUGAL GREECE

Strike days per 1000 employees *1994*
numbers

over 250

100 - 250

50 - 100

25 - 50

below 25

Source: *Zahlen* 1996

The number of strikes in Germany is very low compared with other industrialized nations.

2.5

49.0 | 48.5
civil servants

4.0
13.9
8.0 | 74.1
white collar workers

0.3 | 1.9
9.8
blue collar workers

Union membership *1994* percentages

● DGB
● DBB
● DAG
● CGB

Quelle: *Zahlen* 1996

9.4 million

Members of trade unions *1995*
Source: *Harenberg Lexikon* 1996

1.08 million

0.5 million

0.3 million

Deutscher Gewerkschaftsbund (DGB)

Deutscher Beamtenbund (DBB)

Deutsche Angestellten-Gewerkschaft (DAG)

Christlicher Gewerkschaftsbund (CGB)

Both employees and employers should have the right to organize and the right to have their interests represented.

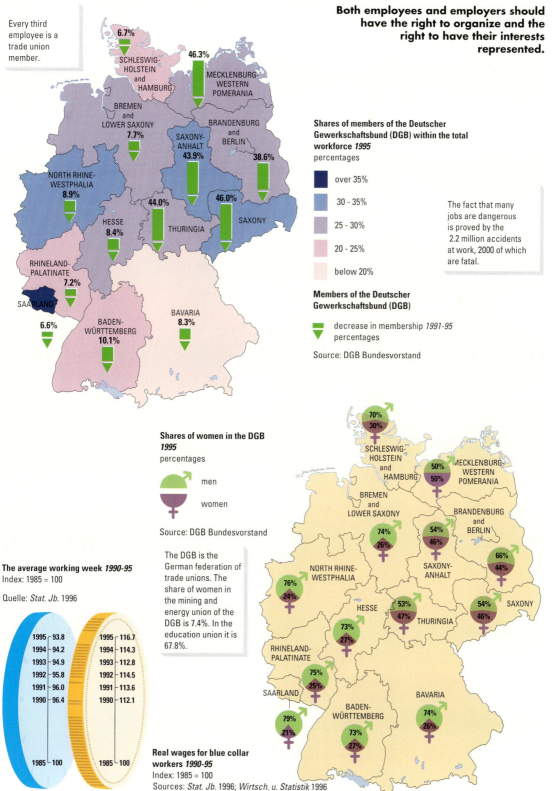

Every third employee is a trade union member.

6.7%
SCHLESWIG-HOLSTEIN and HAMBURG

46.3%
MECKLENBURG-WESTERN POMERANIA

BREMEN and LOWER SAXONY
7.7%

SAXONY-ANHALT
43.9%

BRANDENBURG and BERLIN
38.6%

NORTH RHINE-WESTPHALIA
8.9%

HESSE
8.4%

THURINGIA
44.0%

SAXONY
46.0%

RHINELAND-PALATINATE
7.2%

SAARLAND

6.6%

BADEN-WÜRTTEMBERG
10.1%

BAVARIA
8.3%

Shares of members of the Deutscher Gewerkschaftsbund (DGB) within the total workforce _1995_
percentages

- over 35%
- 30 - 35%
- 25 - 30%
- 20 - 25%
- below 20%

The fact that many jobs are dangerous is proved by the 2.2 million accidents at work, 2000 of which are fatal.

Members of the Deutscher Gewerkschaftsbund (DGB)

decrease in membership _1991-95_ percentages

Source: DGB Bundesvorstand

Shares of women in the DGB _1995_
percentages

men

women

Source: DGB Bundesvorstand

The DGB is the German federation of trade unions. The share of women in the mining and energy union of the DGB is 7.4%. In the education union it is 67.8%.

70% / 30%
SCHLESWIG-HOLSTEIN and HAMBURG

50% / 50%
MECKLENBURG-WESTERN POMERANIA

BREMEN and LOWER SAXONY
74% / 26%

SAXONY-ANHALT
54% / 46%

BRANDENBURG and BERLIN
66% / 44%

NORTH RHINE-WESTPHALIA
76% / 24%

HESSE
73% / 27%

THURINGIA
53% / 47%

SAXONY
54% / 46%

RHINELAND-PALATINATE
75% / 25%

SAARLAND
79% / 21%

BADEN-WÜRTTEMBERG
73% / 27%

BAVARIA
74% / 26%

The average working week _1990-95_
Index: 1985 = 100

Quelle: _Stat. Jb._ 1996

1995 - 93.8	1995 - 116.7
1994 - 94.2	1994 - 114.3
1993 - 94.9	1993 - 112.8
1992 - 95.8	1992 - 114.5
1991 - 96.0	1991 - 113.6
1990 - 96.4	1990 - 112.1
1985 - 100	1985 - 100

Real wages for blue collar workers _1990-95_
Index: 1985 = 100
Sources: _Stat. Jb._ 1996; _Wirtsch. u. Statistik_ 1996

🍀 WORK AND WELFARE

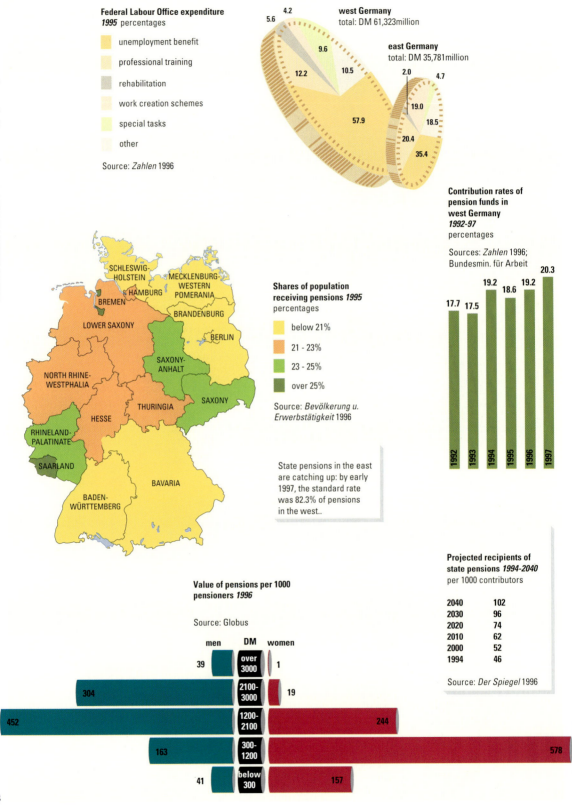

Bernhard Schäfers *The State of Germany Atlas* Copyright © Myriad Editions Limited

Federal Labour Office expenditure
1995 percentages

- unemployment benefit
- professional training
- rehabilitation
- work creation schemes
- special tasks
- other

Source: *Zahlen* 1996

west Germany
total: DM 61,323million

5.6 4.2
9.6
12.2 10.5
57.9

east Germany
total: DM 35,781million

2.0 4.7
19.0
18.5
20.4
35.4

Contribution rates of pension funds in west Germany
1992-97
percentages

Sources: *Zahlen* 1996;
Bundesmin. für Arbeit

1992	1993	1994	1995	1996	1997
17.7	17.5	19.2	18.6	19.2	20.3

Shares of population receiving pensions *1995*
percentages

- below 21%
- 21 - 23%
- 23 - 25%
- over 25%

Source: *Bevölkerung u. Erwerbstätigkeit* 1996

SCHLESWIG-HOLSTEIN
MECKLENBURG-WESTERN POMERANIA
HAMBURG
BREMEN
LOWER SAXONY
BRANDENBURG
BERLIN
NORTH RHINE-WESTPHALIA
SAXONY-ANHALT
HESSE
THURINGIA
SAXONY
RHINELAND-PALATINATE
SAARLAND
BAVARIA
BADEN-WÜRTTEMBERG

State pensions in the east are catching up: by early 1997, the standard rate was 82.3% of pensions in the west..

Projected recipients of state pensions *1994-2040*
per 1000 contributors

2040	102
2030	96
2020	74
2010	62
2000	52
1994	46

Source: *Der Spiegel* 1996

Value of pensions per 1000 pensioners *1996*

Source: Globus

men	DM	women
39	over 3000	1
304	2100-3000	19
452	1200-2100	244
163	300-1200	578
41	below 300	157

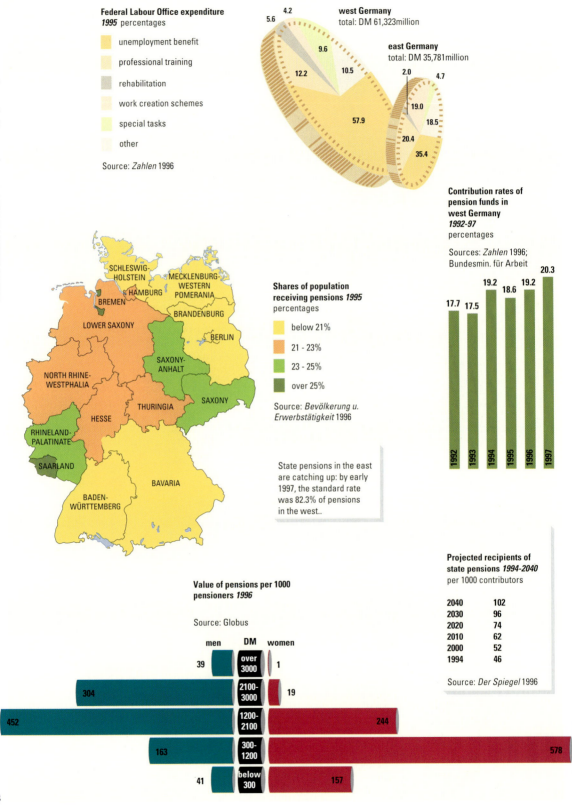

58

It is fundamental to the social state that workers are covered against ill health, accident or invalidity, and are provided for in their old age.

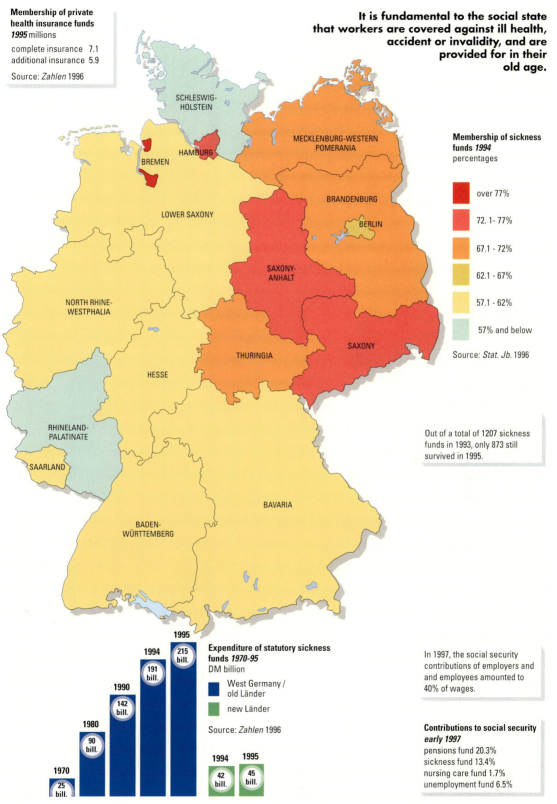

Membership of private health insurance funds
1995 millions

complete insurance   7.1
additional insurance   5.9

Source: *Zahlen* 1996

SCHLESWIG-HOLSTEIN

HAMBURG

BREMEN

MECKLENBURG-WESTERN POMERANIA

LOWER SAXONY

BRANDENBURG

BERLIN

NORTH RHINE-WESTPHALIA

SAXONY-ANHALT

HESSE

THURINGIA

SAXONY

RHINELAND-PALATINATE

SAARLAND

BAVARIA

BADEN-WÜRTTEMBERG

Membership of sickness funds *1994*
percentages

over 77%

72. 1- 77%

67.1 - 72%

62.1 - 67%

57.1 - 62%

57% and below

Source: *Stat. Jb.* 1996

Out of a total of 1207 sickness funds in 1993, only 873 still survived in 1995.

Expenditure of statutory sickness funds *1970-95*
DM billion

1995 — 215 bill.
1994 — 191 bill.
1990 — 142 bill.
1980 — 90 bill.
1970 — 25 bill.

West Germany / old Länder

new Länder

1994 — 42 bill.
1995 — 45 bill.

Source: *Zahlen* 1996

In 1997, the social security contributions of employers and and employees amounted to 40% of wages.

Contributions to social security
early 1997
pensions fund 20.3%
sickness fund 13.4%
nursing care fund 1.7%
unemployment fund 6.5%

Expenditure on benefits for children and young people *1994*

🟥	over 850 DM
🟥	600 - 850
🟩	450 - 600
🟩	375 - 450
🟨	300 - 375
🟨	below 300 DM

Sources: *Stat. Jb.* 1996; *Zahlen* 1996

Germany's social welfare provision is above the EU average, but not the highest.

Germany 31.0%

EU 28.8%

Social welfare spending as proportion of GDP *1993*
percentages

🟪	over 30%	🟦	20 - 25%
🟩	25 - 30%	🟨	below 20%

🔴 increase over 5% since 1980

Source: *Stat. Jb.* 1996

Schleswig-Holstein
Hamburg
Mecklenburg-Western Pomerania
Bremen
Lower Saxony
Brandenburg
Berlin
North Rhine-Westphalia
Saxony-Anhalt
Hesse
Thuringia
Saxony
Rhineland-Palatinate
Saarland
Bavaria
Baden-Württemberg

Since 1970, the federal state has delegated responsibility for the social welfare budget to municipalities and households.

30.4
30.8
0.8 – 8.4
9.6
20.0

Social welfare budget by origin *1994*
percentages

🟨	business
🟨	federal government
🟨	Länder
🟩	municipalities
🟦	households
🟫	other

Source: *Zahlen* 1996

Selected social welfare spending West Germany *1970 and 1980* **Germany** *1992 and 1994* DM billion

🟦	families
🟥	education
🟨	housing
🟥	children/young people
🟩	income support

Source: *Zahlen* 1996

	1970	1980	1992	1994
income support	3.5	15.0	45.9	58.0
children/young people	2.1	8.9	23.3	24.9
housing	0.6	2.0	7.3	6.2
education			7.2	6.7
families	2.9	17.6	21.9	21.0
total spending	**179.2**	**479.8**	**1006.2**	**1106.2**

The willingness of the state to support those in need is a reflection of social attitudes.

Income support is the net beneath the net. It protects against risks not covered by the rest of the welfare system. Its purpose is to ensure that incomes reach subsistence level.

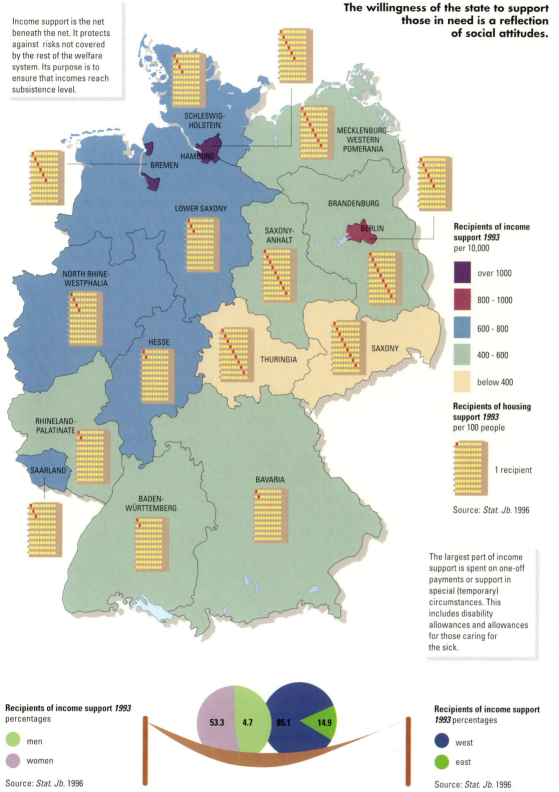

SCHLESWIG-HOLSTEIN

MECKLENBURG-WESTERN POMERANIA

HAMBURG

BREMEN

LOWER SAXONY

BRANDENBURG

NORTH RHINE-WESTPHALIA

SAXONY-ANHALT

BERLIN

HESSE

THURINGIA

SAXONY

RHINELAND-PALATINATE

SAARLAND

BADEN-WÜRTTEMBERG

BAVARIA

Recipients of income support *1993*
per 10,000

over 1000

800 - 1000

600 - 800

400 - 600

below 400

Recipients of housing support *1993*
per 100 people

1 recipient

Source: *Stat. Jb.* 1996

The largest part of income support is spent on one-off payments or support in special (temporary) circumstances. This includes disability allowances and allowances for those caring for the sick.

Recipients of income support *1993*
percentages

men

women

53.3   4.7   85.1   14.9

Source: *Stat. Jb.* 1996

Recipients of income support *1993* percentages

west

east

Source: *Stat. Jb.* 1996

Part Four

THE ECONOMY

Source: Globus 4072/1997

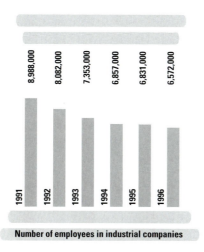

8,988,000   8,082,000   7,353,000   6,857,000   6,831,000   6,572,000

1991   1992   1993   1994   1995   1996

Number of employees in industrial companies

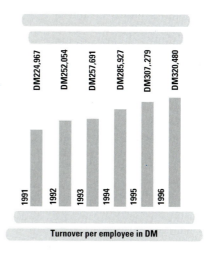

DM224,967   DM252,054   DM257,691   DM285,927   DM307,279   DM320,480

1991   1992   1993   1994   1995   1996

Turnover per employee in DM

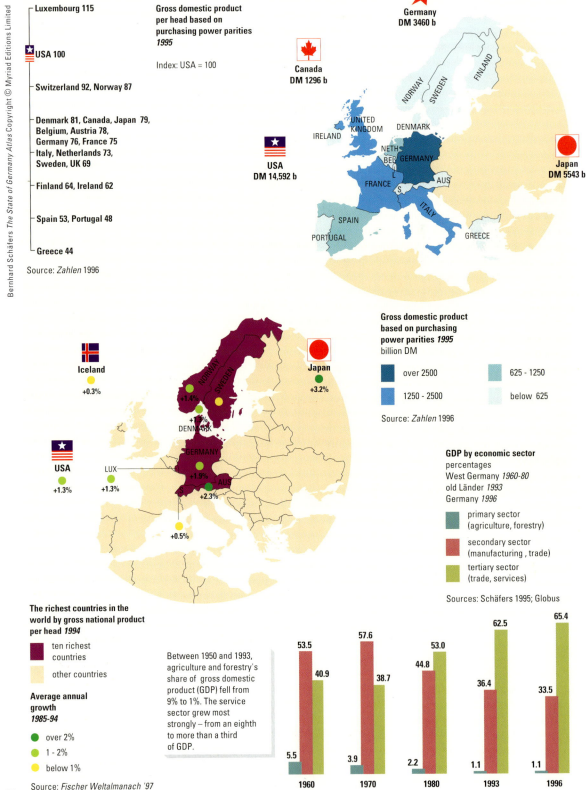

ECONOMY

Bernhard Schäfers *The State of Germany Atlas* Copyright © Myriad Editions Limited

Luxembourg 115

USA 100

Switzerland 92, Norway 87

Denmark 81, Canada, Japan 79,
Belgium, Austria 78,
Germany 76, France 75
Italy, Netherlands 73,
Sweden, UK 69

Finland 64, Ireland 62

Spain 53, Portugal 48

Greece 44

Source: *Zahlen* 1996

**Gross domestic product
per head based on
purchasing power parities**
1995

Index: USA = 100

**Germany
DM 3460 b**

**Canada
DM 1296 b**

**USA
DM 14,592 b**

**Japan
DM 5543 b**

**Gross domestic product
based on purchasing
power parities** *1995*
billion DM

over 2500	625 - 1250
1250 - 2500	below 625

Source: *Zahlen* 1996

Iceland
+0.3%

Japan
+3.2%

NORWAY +1.4%
SWEDEN
+1.9%
DENMARK

GERMANY
+1.9%

USA
+1.3%

LUX
+1.3%

AUS
+2.3%

+0.5%

GDP by economic sector
percentages
West Germany *1960-80*
old Länder *1993*
Germany *1996*

primary sector
(agriculture, forestry)

secondary sector
(manufacturing , trade)

tertiary sector
(trade, services)

Sources: Schäfers 1995; Globus

**The richest countries in the
world by gross national product
per head** *1994*

ten richest
countries

other countries

**Average annual
growth**
1985-94

over 2%

1 - 2%

below 1%

Source: *Fischer Weltalmanach '97*

Between 1950 and 1993,
agriculture and forestry's
share of gross domestic
product (GDP) fell from
9% to 1%. The service
sector grew most
strongly – from an eighth
to more than a third
of GDP.

	1960	1970	1980	1993	1996
primary	5.5	3.9	2.2	1.1	1.1
secondary	53.5	57.6	44.8	36.4	33.5
tertiary	40.9	38.7	53.0	62.5	65.4

**The economy of the new Länder may be
less strong than that of the old Länder
but it has a higher rate of growth.**

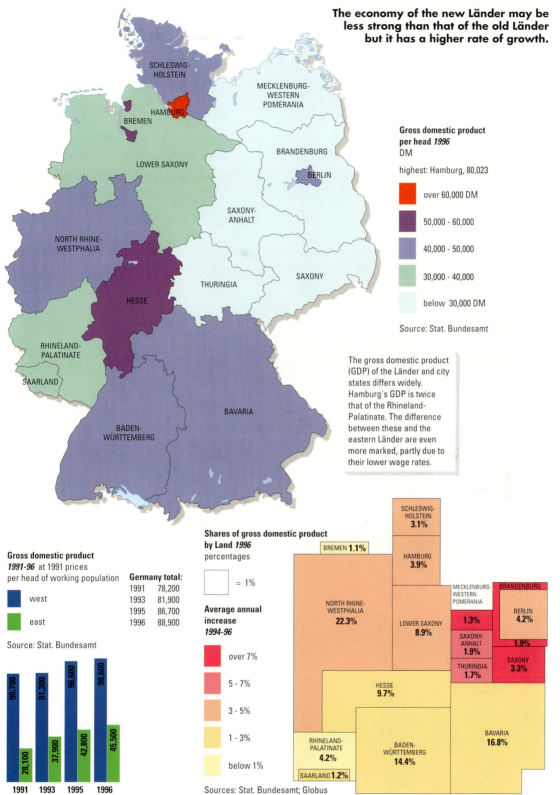

**Gross domestic product
per head *1996*
DM**

highest: Hamburg, 80,023

- over 60,000 DM
- 50,000 - 60,000
- 40,000 - 50,000
- 30,000 - 40,000
- below 30,000 DM

Source: Stat. Bundesamt

The gross domestic product
(GDP) of the Länder and city
states differs widely.
Hamburg's GDP is twice
that of the Rhineland-
Palatinate. The difference
between these and the
eastern Länder are even
more marked, partly due to
their lower wage rates.

Gross domestic product
1991-96 at 1991 prices
per head of working population

Germany total:	
1991	78,200
1993	81,900
1995	86,700
1996	88,900

- west
- east

Source: Stat. Bundesamt

west: 90,700 (1991), 91,300 (1993), 96,600 (1995), 98,600 (1996)
east: 28,100 (1991), 37,900 (1993), 42,800 (1995), 45,500 (1996)

**Shares of gross domestic product
by Land *1996***
percentages

☐ = 1%

**Average annual
increase
1994-96**

- over 7%
- 5 - 7%
- 3 - 5%
- 1 - 3%
- below 1%

BREMEN **1.1%**
SCHLESWIG-HOLSTEIN **3.1%**
HAMBURG **3.9%**
NORTH RHINE-WESTPHALIA **22.3%**
LOWER SAXONY **8.9%**
MECKLENBURG-WESTERN POMERANIA **1.3%**
BRANDENBURG
BERLIN **4.2%**
SAXONY-ANHALT **1.9%**
1.9%
HESSE **9.7%**
THURINGIA **1.7%**
SAXONY **3.3%**
RHINELAND-PALATINATE **4.2%**
BADEN-WÜRTTEMBERG **14.4%**
BAVARIA **16.8%**
SAARLAND **1.2%**

Sources: Stat. Bundesamt; Globus

World's biggest importers *1995*
US$ billion

USA	771
Germany	443
Japan	336
France	273
UK	265
Italy	203
Hong Kong	191
Canada	168
Netherlands	146
South Korea	135

Source: *Fischer Weltalmanach '97*

Imports (excluding re-exports) *1995*

■ most important for Germany

Shares of imports *1995*
over 5%

● over 7.5%

● 5 - 7.4%

Source: *Stat. Jb.* 1996

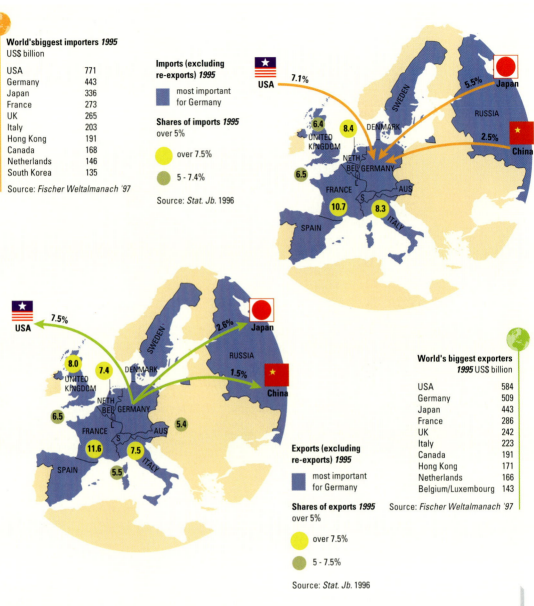

USA 7.1%
Japan 5.5%
China 2.5%
UNITED KINGDOM 6.4
8.4
DENMARK
SWEDEN
RUSSIA
NETH 6.5
BEL GERMANY
FRANCE 10.7
AUS
ITALY 8.3
SPAIN

World's biggest exporters
1995 US$ billion

USA	584
Germany	509
Japan	443
France	286
UK	242
Italy	223
Canada	191
Hong Kong	171
Netherlands	166
Belgium/Luxembourg	143

Source: *Fischer Weltalmanach '97*

USA 7.5%
Japan 2.6%
China 1.5%
UNITED KINGDOM 8.0
7.4
DENMARK
SWEDEN
RUSSIA
NETH 6.5
BEL GERMANY
FRANCE 11.6
AUS 5.4
S 7.5
ITALY
SPAIN 5.5

Exports (excluding re-exports) *1995*

■ most important for Germany

Shares of exports *1995*
over 5%

● over 7.5%

● 5 - 7.5%

Source: *Stat. Jb.* 1996

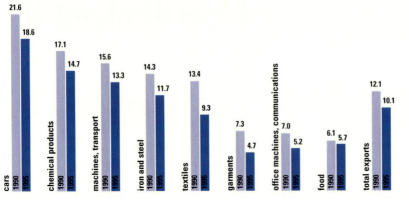

	cars	chemical products	machines, transport	iron and steel	textiles	garments	office machines, communications	food	total exports
1990	21.6	17.1	15.6	14.3	13.4	7.3	7.0	6.1	12.1
1995	18.6	14.7	13.3	11.7	9.3	4.7	5.2	5.7	10.1

In 1996, in spite of rising unemployment, Germany achieved record exports of DM 784 billion, an increase of 5% over the previous year. Exports are the most vital element of the economy.

German exports as a percentage of world exports *1990 and 1995*
percentages

Source: Globus

After the USA, Germany is the largest exporter in the world. Three quarters of its exports go to other EU countries.

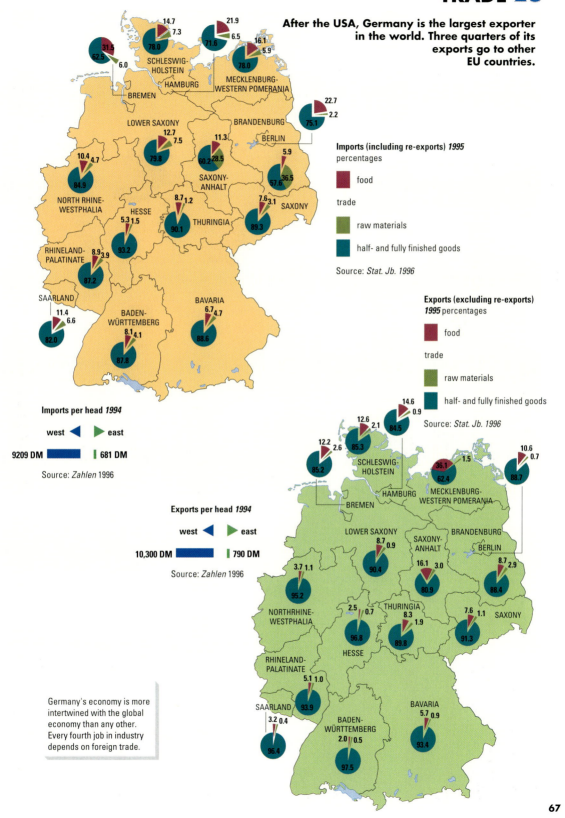

Imports (including re-exports) *1995*
percentages

food

trade

raw materials

half- and fully finished goods

Source: *Stat. Jb. 1996*

Exports (excluding re-exports)
1995 percentages

food

trade

raw materials

half- and fully finished goods

Source: *Stat. Jb. 1996*

Imports per head *1994*

west ◀ ▶ east

9209 DM | 681 DM

Source: *Zahlen* 1996

Exports per head *1994*

west ◀ ▶ east

10,300 DM | 790 DM

Source: *Zahlen* 1996

Germany's economy is more intertwined with the global economy than any other. Every fourth job in industry depends on foreign trade.

Imports map labels:
SCHLESWIG-HOLSTEIN 14.7 / 7.3 / 78.0
HAMBURG 21.9 / 6.5 / 71.6
BREMEN 31.5 / 6.0 / 62.5
MECKLENBURG-WESTERN POMERANIA 16.1 / 5.9 / 78.0
LOWER SAXONY 12.7 / 7.5 / 79.8
BRANDENBURG 11.3 / 28.5 / 60.2
BERLIN 22.7 / 2.2 / 75.1
NORTH RHINE-WESTPHALIA 10.4 / 4.7 / 84.9
SAXONY-ANHALT 5.9 / 36.5 / 57.6
HESSE 8.7 / 1.2 / 90.1
THURINGIA 5.3 / 1.5 / 93.2
SAXONY 7.6 / 3.1 / 89.3
RHINELAND-PALATINATE 8.9 / 3.9 / 87.2
SAARLAND 11.4 / 6.6 / 82.0
BADEN-WÜRTTEMBERG 8.1 / 4.1 / 87.8
BAVARIA 6.7 / 4.7 / 88.6

Exports map labels:
BREMEN 12.2 / 2.6 / 85.2
SCHLESWIG-HOLSTEIN 12.6 / 2.1 / 85.3
HAMBURG 14.6 / 0.9 / 84.5
MECKLENBURG-WESTERN POMERANIA 36.1 / 1.5 / 62.4
BERLIN 10.6 / 0.7 / 88.7
LOWER SAXONY 8.7 / 0.9 / 90.4
SAXONY-ANHALT 16.1 / 3.0 / 80.9
BRANDENBURG 8.7 / 2.9 / 88.4
NORTHRHINE-WESTPHALIA 3.7 / 1.1 / 95.2
THURINGIA 8.3 / 1.9 / 89.8
HESSE 2.5 / 0.7 / 96.8
SAXONY 7.6 / 1.1 / 91.3
RHINELAND-PALATINATE 5.1 / 1.0 / 93.9
SAARLAND 3.2 / 0.4 / 96.4
BADEN-WÜRTTEMBERG 2.0 / 0.5 / 97.5
BAVARIA 5.7 / 0.9 / 93.4

Bernhard Schäfers *The State of Germany Atlas* Copyright © Myriad Editions Limited

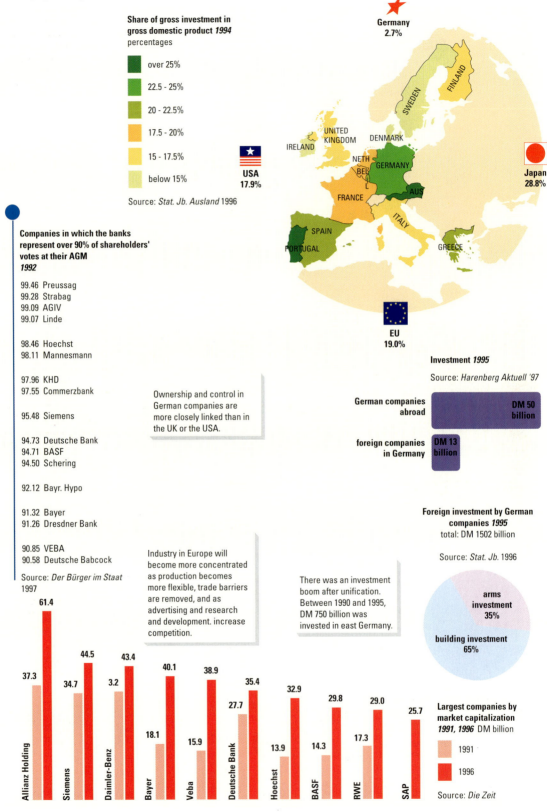

Share of gross investment in gross domestic product *1994*
percentages

- over 25%
- 22.5 - 25%
- 20 - 22.5%
- 17.5 - 20%
- 15 - 17.5%
- below 15%

Source: *Stat. Jb. Ausland* 1996

USA 17.9%

Germany 2.7%

Japan 28.8%

EU 19.0%

Companies in which the banks represent over 90% of shareholders' votes at their AGM *1992*

99.46 Preussag
99.28 Strabag
99.09 AGIV
99.07 Linde

98.46 Hoechst
98.11 Mannesmann

97.96 KHD
97.55 Commerzbank

95.48 Siemens

94.73 Deutsche Bank
94.71 BASF
94.50 Schering

92.12 Bayr. Hypo

91.32 Bayer
91.26 Dresdner Bank

90.85 VEBA
90.58 Deutsche Babcock

Source: *Der Bürger im Staat* 1997

Ownership and control in German companies are more closely linked than in the UK or the USA.

Industry in Europe will become more concentrated as production becomes more flexible, trade barriers are removed, and as advertising and research and development. increase competition.

There was an investment boom after unification. Between 1990 and 1995, DM 750 billion was invested in east Germany.

Investment *1995*

Source: *Harenberg Aktuell '97*

German companies abroad — **DM 50 billion**

foreign companies in Germany — **DM 13 billion**

Foreign investment by German companies *1995*
total: DM 1502 billion

Source: *Stat. Jb.* 1996

- arms investment 35%
- building investment 65%

Largest companies by market capitalization *1991, 1996* DM billion

- 1991
- 1996

Source: *Die Zeit*

Company	1991	1996
Allianz Holding	37.3	61.4
Siemens	34.7	44.5
Daimler-Benz	3.2	43.4
Bayer	18.1	40.1
Veba	15.9	38.9
Deutsche Bank	27.7	35.4
Hoechst	13.9	32.9
BASF	14.3	29.8
RWE	17.3	29.0
SAP	—	25.7

The economy depends not just on the big industrial companies but on a complex finance and insurance network and on international speculation.

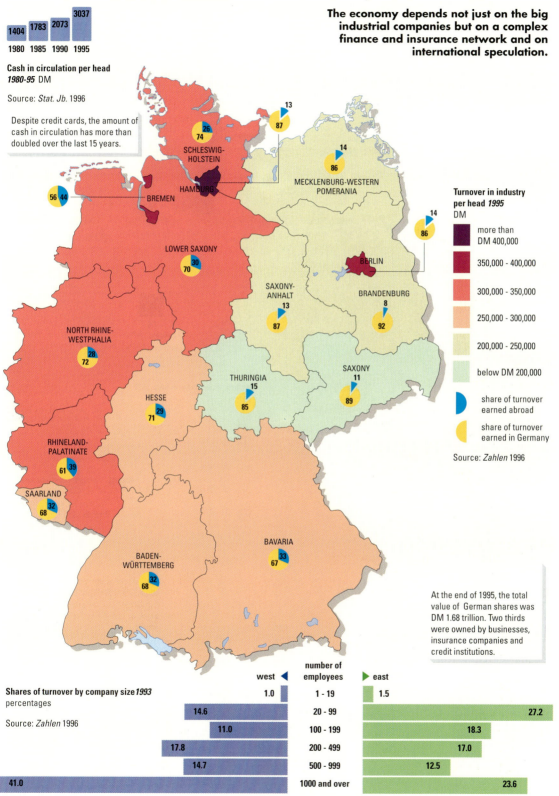

1404	1783	2073	3037
1980	1985	1990	1995

Cash in circulation per head
1980-95 DM

Source: *Stat. Jb.* 1996

Despite credit cards, the amount of cash in circulation has more than doubled over the last 15 years.

SCHLESWIG-HOLSTEIN 26 / 74 — 13 / 87

MECKLENBURG-WESTERN POMERANIA 14 / 86

HAMBURG — BREMEN 56 / 44

LOWER SAXONY 30 / 70

BERLIN 14 / 86

SAXONY-ANHALT 13 / 87

BRANDENBURG 8 / 92

NORTH RHINE-WESTPHALIA 28 / 72

THURINGIA 15 / 85

SAXONY 11 / 89

HESSE 29 / 71

RHINELAND-PALATINATE 61 / 39

SAARLAND 32 / 68

BADEN-WÜRTTEMBERG 68 / 32

BAVARIA 33 / 67

Turnover in industry per head *1995* DM

- more than DM 400,000
- 350,000 - 400,000
- 300,000 - 350,000
- 250,000 - 300,000
- 200,000 - 250,000
- below DM 200,000
- share of turnover earned abroad
- share of turnover earned in Germany

Source: *Zahlen* 1996

At the end of 1995, the total value of German shares was DM 1.68 trillion. Two thirds were owned by businesses, insurance companies and credit institutions.

Shares of turnover by company size *1993*
percentages

Source: *Zahlen* 1996

west ◀	number of employees	▶ east
1.0	1 - 19	1.5
14.6	20 - 99	27.2
11.0	100 - 199	18.3
17.8	200 - 499	17.0
14.7	500 - 999	12.5
41.0	1000 and over	23.6

Bernhard Schäfers *The State of Germany Atlas* Copyright © Myriad Editions Limited

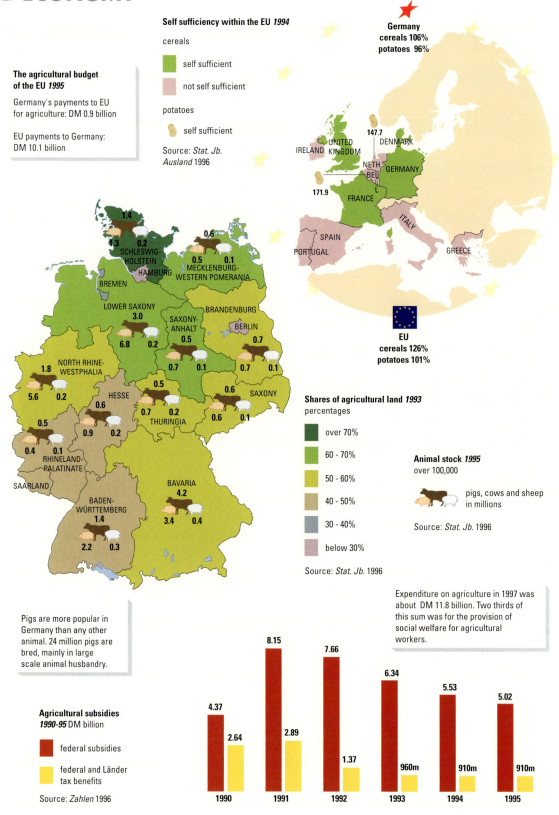

Self sufficiency within the EU *1994*

cereals

- self sufficient
- not self sufficient

potatoes

- self sufficient

Source: *Stat. Jb. Ausland* 1996

**Germany
cereals 106%
potatoes 96%**

**The agricultural budget
of the EU** *1995*

Germany's payments to EU
for agriculture: DM 0.9 billion

EU payments to Germany:
DM 10.1 billion

IRELAND
UNITED KINGDOM
147.7
DENMARK
NETH
BEL
L
GERMANY
171.9
FRANCE
ITALY
SPAIN
PORTUGAL
GREECE

**EU
cereals 126%
potatoes 101%**

SCHLESWIG-HOLSTEIN 1.4 / 1.3 / 0.2 / 0.5 / 0.1
HAMBURG
MECKLENBURG-WESTERN POMERANIA 0.6 / 0.5 / 0.1
BREMEN
LOWER SAXONY 3.0 / 6.8 / 0.2
BRANDENBURG
BERLIN
SAXONY-ANHALT 0.5 / 0.7 / 0.1
0.7 / 0.7 / 0.1
NORTH RHINE-WESTPHALIA 1.8 / 5.6 / 0.2
HESSE 0.6 / 0.7 / 0.2
THURINGIA 0.5
SAXONY 0.6 / 0.6 / 0.1
0.5 / 0.9 / 0.2
0.4 / 0.1
RHINELAND-PALATINATE
SAARLAND
BADEN-WÜRTTEMBERG 1.4 / 2.2 / 0.3
BAVARIA 4.2 / 3.4 / 0.4

Shares of agricultural land *1993*
percentages

- over 70%
- 60 - 70%
- 50 - 60%
- 40 - 50%
- 30 - 40%
- below 30%

Source: *Stat. Jb.* 1996

Animal stock *1995*
over 100,000

pigs, cows and sheep
in millions

Source: *Stat. Jb.* 1996

Pigs are more popular in
Germany than any other
animal. 24 million pigs are
bred, mainly in large
scale animal husbandry.

Expenditure on agriculture in 1997 was
about DM 11.8 billion. Two thirds of
this sum was for the provision of
social welfare for agricultural
workers.

Agricultural subsidies
1990-95 DM billion

- federal subsidies
- federal and Länder
  tax benefits

Source: *Zahlen* 1996

Year	federal subsidies	federal and Länder tax benefits
1990	4.37	2.64
1991	8.15	2.89
1992	7.66	1.37
1993	6.34	960m
1994	5.53	910m
1995	5.02	910m

Almost half of Germany's land is given over to agriculture, but it employs only 3 percent of the fulltime workforce.

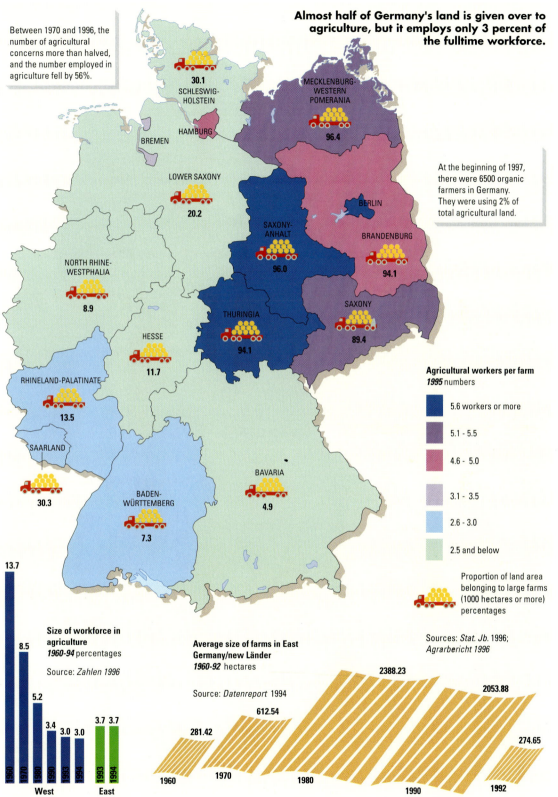

Between 1970 and 1996, the number of agricultural concerns more than halved, and the number employed in agriculture fell by 56%.

At the beginning of 1997, there were 6500 organic farmers in Germany. They were using 2% of total agricultural land.

SCHLESWIG-HOLSTEIN
30.1

HAMBURG

BREMEN

MECKLENBURG-WESTERN POMERANIA
96.4

LOWER SAXONY
20.2

BERLIN

SAXONY-ANHALT
96.0

BRANDENBURG
94.1

NORTH RHINE-WESTPHALIA
8.9

THURINGIA
94.1

SAXONY
89.4

HESSE
11.7

RHINELAND-PALATINATE
13.5

SAARLAND
30.3

BADEN-WÜRTTEMBERG
7.3

BAVARIA
4.9

Agricultural workers per farm
1995 numbers

- 5.6 workers or more
- 5.1 - 5.5
- 4.6 - 5.0
- 3.1 - 3.5
- 2.6 - 3.0
- 2.5 and below

Proportion of land area belonging to large farms (1000 hectares or more) percentages

Sources: *Stat. Jb.* 1996; *Agrarbericht* 1996

Size of workforce in agriculture
1960-94 percentages

Source: *Zahlen 1996*

13.7 | 8.5 | 5.2 | 3.4 | 3.0 | 3.0 | 3.7 | 3.7
1960 | 1970 | 1980 | 1990 | 1993 | 1994 | 1993 | 1994
West | **East**

Average size of farms in East Germany/new Länder
1960-92 hectares

Source: *Datenreport* 1994

281.42 — 1960
612.54 — 1970
2388.23 — 1980
2053.88 — 1990
274.65 — 1992

71

 ECONOMY

Nuclear power stations
1996

29 number in operation
or under construction

1 unsafe or dangerous in 1993,
2 according to International
Atomic Energy Authority

Sources: *Harenberg Aktuell '97;
Der Öko-Atlas*

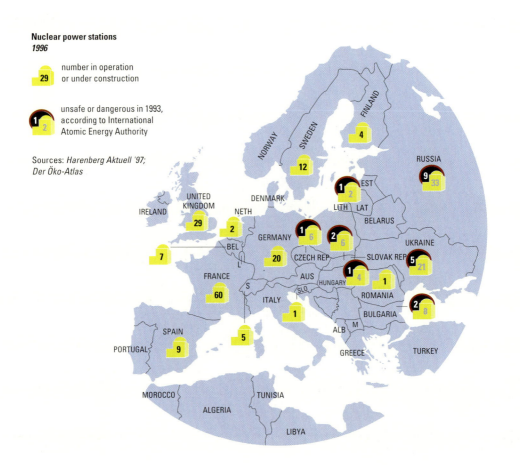

Primary energy use worldwide *1994*
tonnes oil equivalent (toe)

- over 7 toe
- 5 - 7
- 3 - 5
- 1 - 3
- below 1 toe
- other states

Source: *Stat. Jb. Ausland* 1996

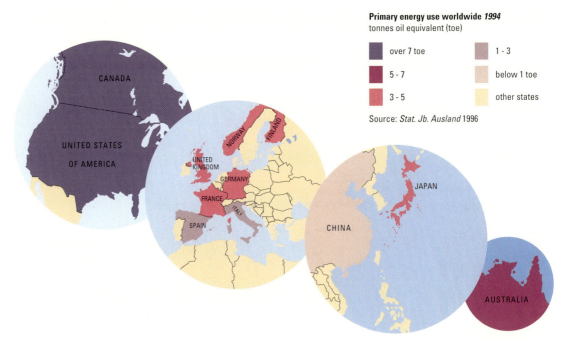

Energy is essential for survival but however efficient its use, it causes some damage to the environment.

Germany produces more lignite than any other country in the world. It is the 9th largest producer of natural gas and the 19th of hard coal.

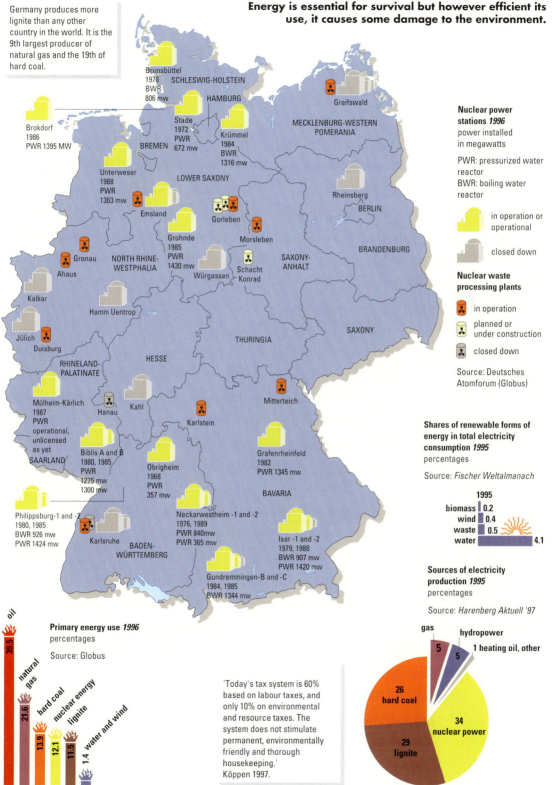

SCHLESWIG-HOLSTEIN

Brunsbüttel
1976
BWR
806 mw

HAMBURG

Greifswald

MECKLENBURG-WESTERN POMERANIA

Stade
1972
PWR

Krümmel
1984
BWR
1316 mw

Brokdorf
1986
PWR 1395 MW

BREMEN

LOWER SAXONY

Unterweser
1988
PWR
1363 mw

Rheinsberg

Emsland

Gorleben

BERLIN

Grohnde
1985
PWR
1430 mw

Morsleben

BRANDENBURG

Gronau

NORTH RHINE-WESTPHALIA

Ahaus

Würgassen

Schacht
Konrad

SAXONY-ANHALT

Kalkar

Hamm Uentrop

SAXONY

Jülich

Duisburg

THURINGIA

RHINELAND-PALATINATE

HESSE

Mülheim-Kärlich
1987
PWR
operational,
unlicensed
as yet

Hanau

Kahl

Mitterteich

Karlstein

SAARLAND

Biblis A and B
1980, 1985
PWR
1225 mw
1300 mw

Obrigheim
1968
PWR
357 mw

Grafenrheinfeld
1982
PWR 1345 mw

Philippsburg-1 and -2
1980, 1985
BWR 926 mw
PWR 1424 mw

Karlsruhe

BADEN-WÜRTTEMBERG

Neckarwestheim -1 and -2
1976, 1989
PWR 840mw
PWR 365mw

Isar -1 and -2
1979, 1988
BWR 907 mw
PWR 1420 mw

BAVARIA

Gundremmingen-B and -C
1984, 1985
BWR 1344 mw

Nuclear power stations *1996*
power installed
in megawatts

PWR: pressurized water reactor
BWR: boiling water reactor

- in operation or operational
- closed down

Nuclear waste processing plants

- in operation
- planned or under construction
- closed down

Source: Deutsches Atomforum (Globus)

Shares of renewable forms of energy in total electricity consumption *1995*
percentages

Source: *Fischer Weltalmanach*

	1995
biomass	0.2
wind	0.4
waste	0.5
water	4.1

Sources of electricity production *1995*
percentages

Source: *Harenberg Aktuell '97*

gas — 5
hydropower — 5
1 heating oil, other

26 hard coal
34 nuclear power
29 lignite

Primary energy use *1996*
percentages

Source: Globus

oil — 39.5
natural gas — 21.6
hard coal — 13.9
nuclear energy — 12.1
lignite — 11.5
water and wind — 1.4

'Today's tax system is 60% based on labour taxes, and only 10% on environmental and resource taxes. The system does not stimulate permanent, environmentally friendly and thorough housekeeping.'
Köppen 1997.

Bernhard Schäfers *The State of Germany Atlas* Copyright © Myriad Editions Limited

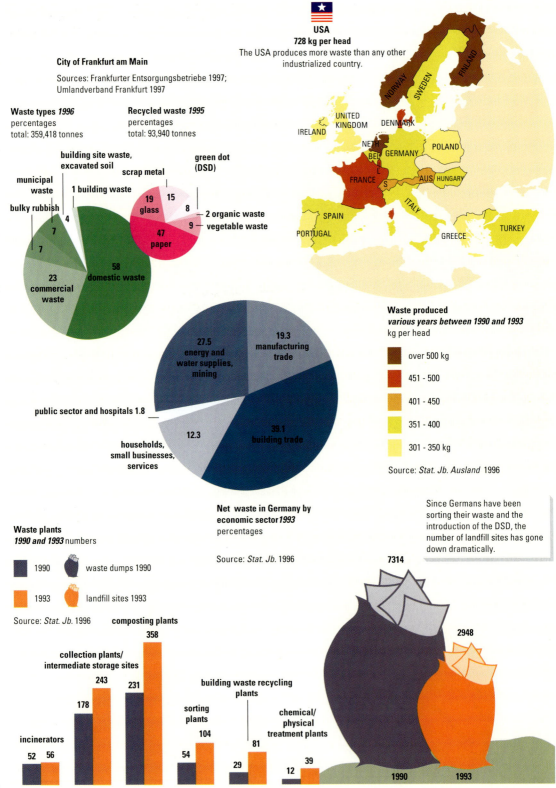

City of Frankfurt am Main

Sources: Frankfurter Entsorgungsbetriebe 1997;
Umlandverband Frankfurt 1997

Waste types *1996*
percentages
total: 359,418 tonnes

Recycled waste *1995*
percentages
total: 93,940 tonnes

building site waste,
excavated soil

scrap metal

green dot
(DSD)

municipal
waste

1 building waste

bulky rubbish

4

7

7

23
commercial
waste

58
domestic waste

19
glass

15

8

47
paper

9

2 organic waste

vegetable waste

USA
728 kg per head
The USA produces more waste than any other
industrialized country.

NORWAY
SWEDEN
FINLAND
IRELAND
UNITED KINGDOM
DENMARK
NETH
BEL
L
GERMANY
POLAND
FRANCE
S
AUS
HUNGARY
SPAIN
ITALY
PORTUGAL
GREECE
TURKEY

Waste produced
various years between 1990 and 1993
kg per head

- over 500 kg
- 451 - 500
- 401 - 450
- 351 - 400
- 301 - 350 kg

Source: *Stat. Jb. Ausland* 1996

27.5
energy and
water supplies,
mining

19.3
manufacturing
trade

public sector and hospitals 1.8

12.3

39.1
building trade

households,
small businesses,
services

**Net waste in Germany by
economic sector** *1993*
percentages

Source: *Stat. Jb.* 1996

Since Germans have been
sorting their waste and the
introduction of the DSD, the
number of landfill sites has gone
down dramatically.

Waste plants
1990 and 1993 numbers

- 1990
- 1993
- waste dumps 1990
- landfill sites 1993

Source: *Stat. Jb.* 1996

7314

2948

composting plants
358

collection plants/
intermediate storage sites
243

231

178

building waste recycling
plants

sorting
plants

104

chemical/
physical
treatment plants

81

incinerators

52   56

54

29

12   39

1990

1993

Industrial production and mass consumption have a direct impact on the type and quantity of waste produced.

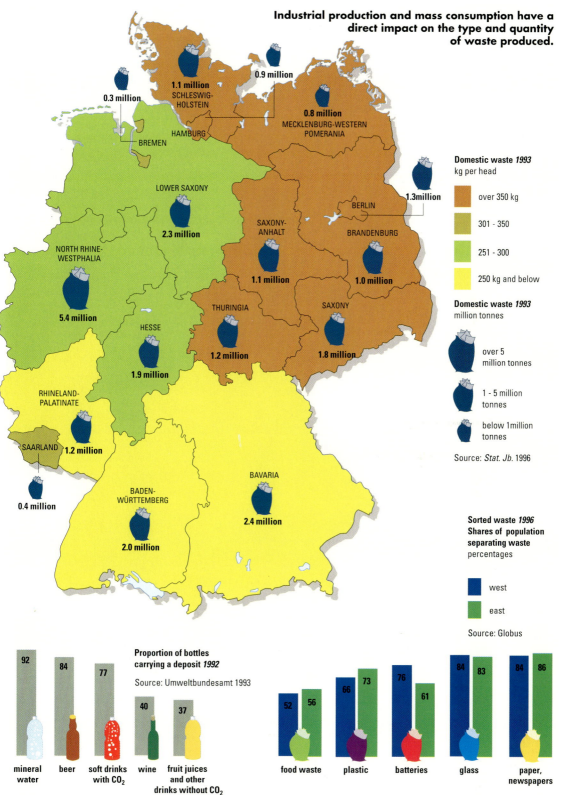

0.3 million

1.1 million
SCHLESWIG-HOLSTEIN

0.9 million

0.8 million
MECKLENBURG-WESTERN POMERANIA

HAMBURG

BREMEN

LOWER SAXONY

2.3 million

1.3 million

BERLIN

NORTH RHINE-WESTPHALIA

5.4 million

SAXONY-ANHALT

1.1 million

BRANDENBURG

1.0 million

HESSE

1.9 million

THURINGIA

1.2 million

SAXONY

1.8 million

RHINELAND-PALATINATE

SAARLAND 1.2 million

0.4 million

BAVARIA

2.4 million

BADEN-WÜRTTEMBERG

2.0 million

Domestic waste *1993*
kg per head

- over 350 kg
- 301 - 350
- 251 - 300
- 250 kg and below

Domestic waste *1993*
million tonnes

- over 5 million tonnes
- 1 - 5 million tonnes
- below 1 million tonnes

Source: *Stat. Jb.* 1996

Sorted waste *1996*
Shares of population separating waste
percentages

- west
- east

Source: Globus

Proportion of bottles carrying a deposit *1992*

Source: Umweltbundesamt 1993

92	mineral water
84	beer
77	soft drinks with CO_2
40	wine
37	fruit juices and other drinks without CO_2

	west	east
food waste	52	56
plastic	66	73
batteries	76	61
glass	84	83
paper, newspapers	84	86

Part Five

THE STATE AND POLITICS

West Germany (former FRG)

1949 OEEC: since 1961 OECD

1951 Council of Europe

1952 World Bank

1954 Western European Union (WEU)

1955 NATO

1955 Organizations of the UN (eg UNICEF, ILO)

1973 UN

Membership of international organizations

East Germany (DDR)

1955 Warsaw Pact

1973 UN

Since unification on 3 October 1990, West Germany's memberships have applied to all Germany.

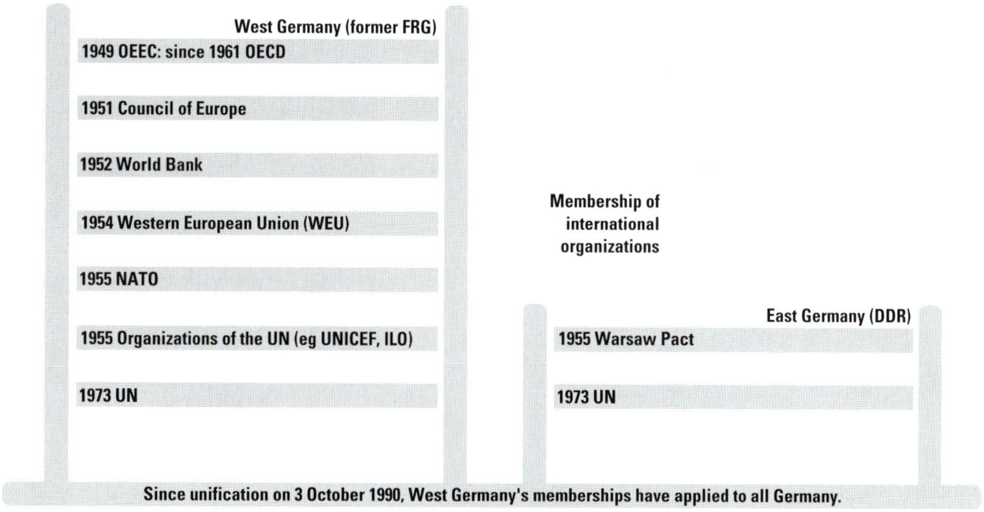

Source: Schäfers 1997

The German state
Source: Erich Schmidt Verlag

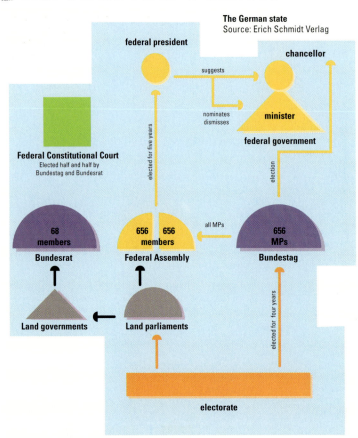

federal president

chancellor

suggests

nominates
dismisses

minister

federal government

elected for five years

Federal Constitutional Court
Elected half and half by
Bundestag and Bundesrat

68
members

Bundesrat

656   656
members

Federal Assembly

all MPs

election

656
MPs

Bundestag

elected for four years

Land governments

Land parliaments

electorate

**Administrative districts in
East Germany (GDR)
*to 3 October 1990***

The Federal Republic of Germany came into
being with ratification of the Basic Law
on 22 May 1949. Since unification with
the GDR on 3 October 1990, people talk
of the 'old' and 'new' Länder.

'Being a German citizen is fairly abstract.
People are first of all Thuringians,
Bavarians, Westphalians or East
Friesians.' Bernhard Vogel,
President of Thuringia, 3 October 1996

**Number of Bundesrat
members per Land** *1996*

1 member

total: 68 members

Source: *Jb. d. Br.* 1996

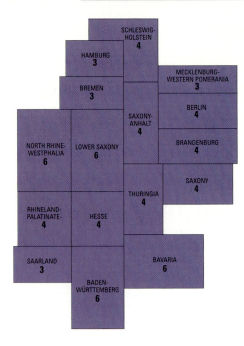

**Länder shares in the
13th Bundestag
*1994-98***

10 seats

Total: 656 and 16 seats

Source: *Stat. Jb.* 1996

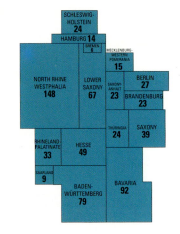

On 20 June 1991, the Bundestag decided, by a small majority, to make Berlin once more the capital of Germany and that the Bundestag itself should move there. By 1997, only the federal president had moved to Berlin. The Bundestag and the Bundesrat are due to move in 1999.

Germany has been shaped by the principles of federalism and by the German constitution, or Basic Law.

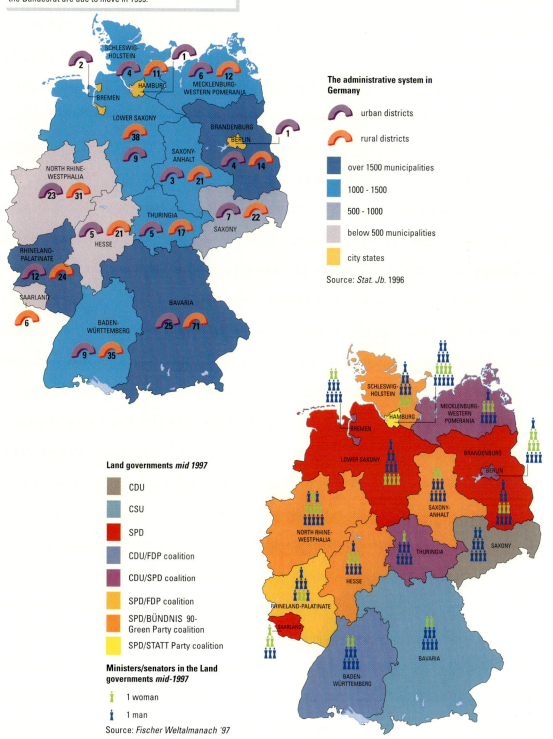

The administrative system in Germany

- urban districts
- rural districts
- over 1500 municipalities
- 1000 - 1500
- 500 - 1000
- below 500 municipalities
- city states

Source: *Stat. Jb.* 1996

Land governments *mid 1997*

- CDU
- CSU
- SPD
- CDU/FDP coalition
- CDU/SPD coalition
- SPD/FDP coalition
- SPD/BÜNDNIS 90-Green Party coalition
- SPD/STATT Party coalition

Ministers/senators in the Land governments *mid-1997*

- 1 woman
- 1 man

Source: *Fischer Weltalmanach '97*

Bernhard Schäfers *The State of Germany Atlas* Copyright © Myriad Editions Limited

Shares of votes of leading parties in European Parliament elections
1994

CDU/CSU majority

☐ below 42%

☐ 42% and above

SPD majority

☐ below 42%

☐ 42% and above

Source: *Stat. Jb.* 1995

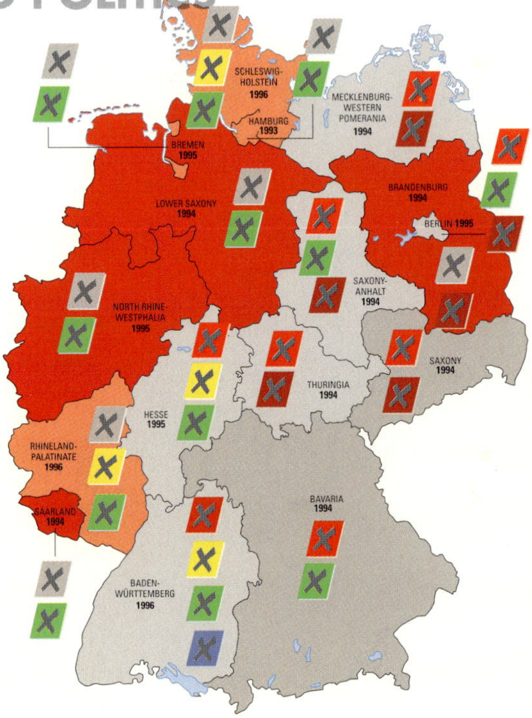

Shares of votes of leading parties in the latest Landtag elections
1993-96

CDU/CSU majority

☐ below 42%

☐ 42% and above

SPD majority

☐ below 42%

☐ 42% and above

All other parties in the Landtag: parties with over 5% of vote

✗ CDU/CSU

✗ SPD

✗ FDP

✗ Bündnis 90/ Green Party

✗ PDS

✗ REP

Source: *Fischer Weltalmanach '97*

Map labels (main map):
SCHLESWIG-HOLSTEIN 1996
HAMBURG 1993
BREMEN 1995
MECKLENBURG-WESTERN POMERANIA 1994
LOWER SAXONY 1994
BRANDENBURG 1994
BERLIN 1995
NORTH RHINE-WESTPHALIA 1995
SAXONY-ANHALT 1994
SAXONY 1994
THURINGIA 1994
HESSE 1995
RHINELAND-PALATINATE 1996
SAARLAND 1994
BADEN-WÜRTTEMBERG 1996
BAVARIA 1994

Map labels (small map):
Schleswig-Holstein, Hamburg, Bremen, Mecklenburg-Western Pomerania, Lower Saxony, Brandenburg, Berlin, North Rhine-Westphalia, Saxony-Anhalt, Saxony, Thuringia, Hesse, Rhineland-Palatinate, Saarland, Baden-Württemberg, Bavaria

Socialist group
40 Germany
63 UK
22 Spain
18 Italy
15 France
221 EU total

Green Group
12 Germany
4 Italy
25 EU total

European Democratic Alliance
9 Spain
7 France
5 Italy
31 EU total

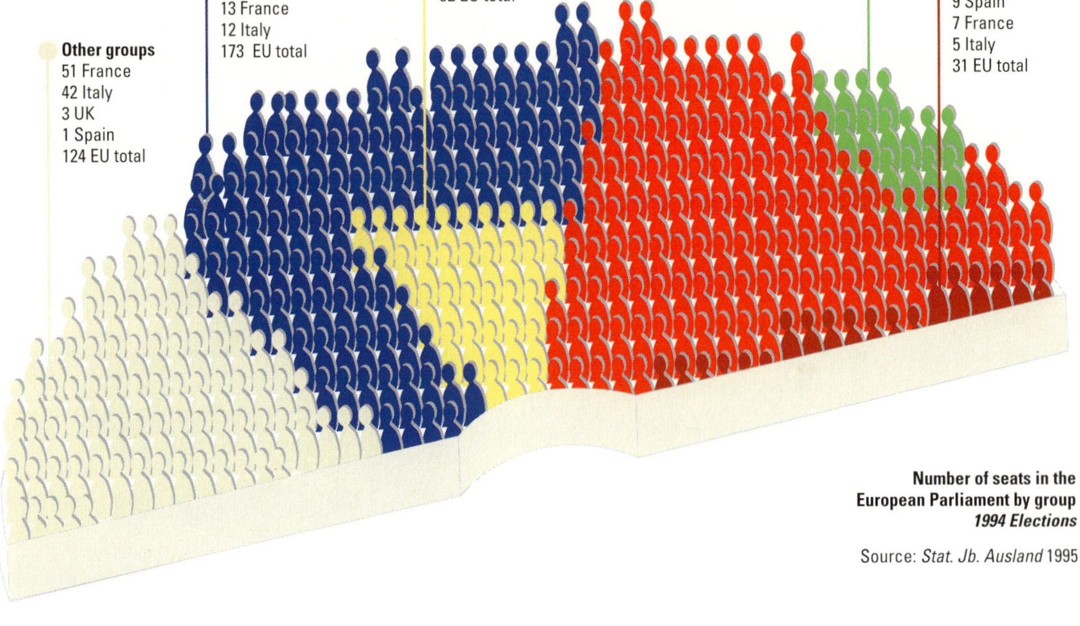

Group of European People's Parties
(Christian democrat)
47 Germany
30 Spain
19 UK
13 France
12 Italy
173 EU total

Liberal, democratic and reformist group
6 Italy
2 UK
2 Spain
1 France
52 EU total

Other groups
51 France
42 Italy
3 UK
1 Spain
124 EU total

Number of seats in the European Parliament by group
1994 Elections

Source: *Stat. Jb. Ausland* 1995

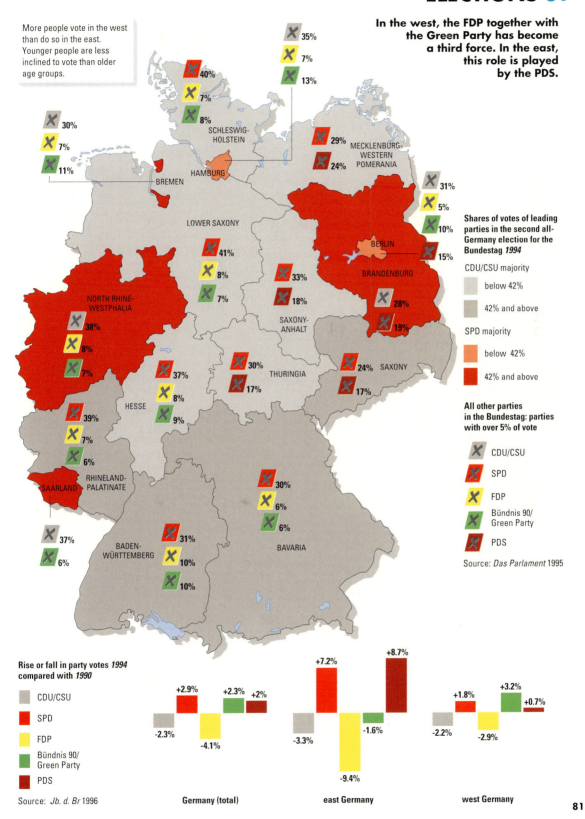

In the west, the FDP together with the Green Party has become a third force. In the east, this role is played by the PDS.

More people vote in the west than do so in the east. Younger people are less inclined to vote than older age groups.

SCHLESWIG-HOLSTEIN

35%
7%
13%

40%
7%
8%

HAMBURG

30%
7%
11%

BREMEN

MECKLENBURG-WESTERN POMERANIA

29%
24%

31%
5%
10%
15%

LOWER SAXONY

41%
8%
7%

BERLIN

BRANDENBURG

28%
19%

NORTH RHINE-WESTPHALIA

38%
8%
7%

SAXONY-ANHALT

33%
18%

HESSE

37%
8%
9%

THURINGIA

30%
17%

SAXONY

24%
17%

SAARLAND

39%
7%
6%

RHINELAND-PALATINATE

37%
6%

BADEN-WÜRTTEMBERG

31%
10%
10%

BAVARIA

30%
6%
6%

Shares of votes of leading parties in the second all-Germany election for the Bundestag *1994*

CDU/CSU majority

below 42%

42% and above

SPD majority

below 42%

42% and above

All other parties in the Bundestag: parties with over 5% of vote

CDU/CSU

SPD

FDP

Bündnis 90/ Green Party

PDS

Source: *Das Parlament* 1995

Rise or fall in party votes *1994* compared with *1990*

CDU/CSU

SPD

FDP

Bündnis 90/ Green Party

PDS

Germany (total)

-2.3%
+2.9%
-4.1%
+2.3%
+2%

east Germany

-3.3%
+7.2%
-9.4%
-1.6%
+8.7%

west Germany

-2.2%
+1.8%
-2.9%
+3.2%
+0.7%

Source: *Jb. d. Br* 1996

**Membership of the
two large parties** *1995*
percentages

Source: *Fischer Weltalmanach '97*

- white collar workers
- blue collar workers
- civil servants
- farmers
- pensioners
- self employed

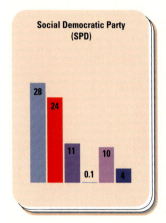

**Social Democratic Party
(SPD)**

28 24 11 0.1 10 4

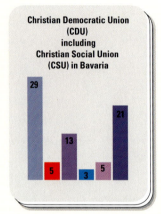

**Christian Democratic Union
(CDU)
including
Christian Social Union
(CSU) in Bavaria**

29 5 13 3 5 21

**Shares of party members
who are women** *1995*
percentages

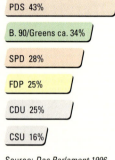

PDS 43%
B. 90/Greens ca. 34%
SPD 28%
FDP 25%
CDU 25%
CSU 16%

Source: *Das Parlament 1996*

177 or 26% of the 672
MPs in the 13th
Bundestag are women.
Parties with explicit
policies on women and
rules on quotas have the
highest number of
women MPs.

Party incomes *1993*
percentages

Source: Bundestagdrucksache

- membership
- donations
- election campaign reimbursement
- other

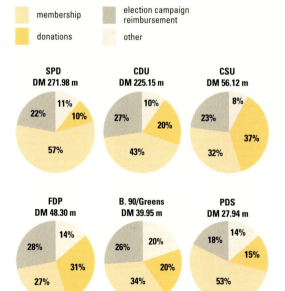

SPD
DM 271.98 m
11% 10% 22% 57%

CDU
DM 225.15 m
10% 20% 27% 43%

CSU
DM 56.12 m
8% 37% 23% 32%

FDP
DM 48.30 m
14% 31% 28% 27%

B. 90/Greens
DM 39.95 m
20% 20% 26% 34%

PDS
DM 27.94 m
14% 15% 18% 53%

**Members of right wing extremist
parties** *1990-94*
rise or fall in numbers

Source: *Verfassungsschutzbericht*

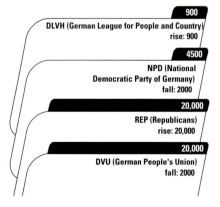

900
DLVH (German League for People and Country)
rise: 900

4500
**NPD (National
Democratic Party of Germany)**
fall: 2000

20,000
REP (Republicans)
rise: 20,000

20,000
DVU (German People's Union)
fall: 2000

Unification has changed both the party landscape and the ruling alliances.

In the 1994 federal elections, the highest vote of people below the age of 44 went to the SPD; the highest vote of people 45 and over went to the CDU/CSU.

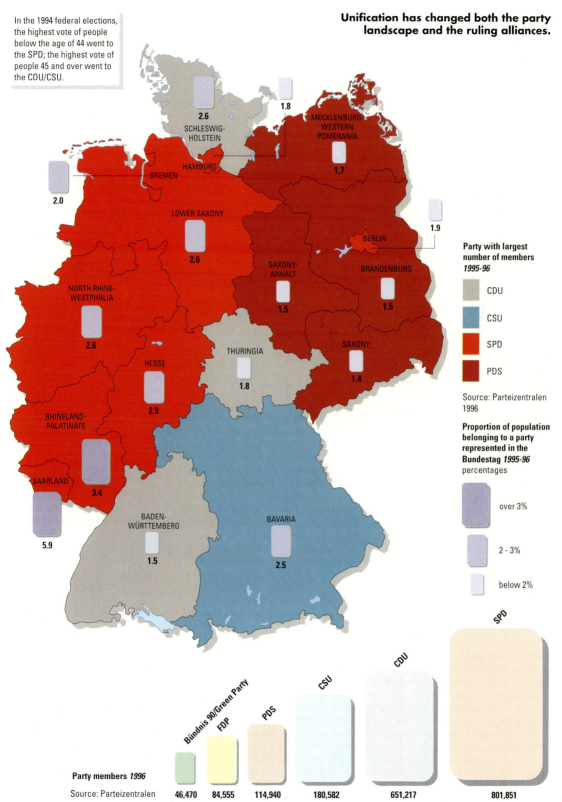

SCHLESWIG-HOLSTEIN **2.6**

1.8

MECKLENBURG-WESTERN POMERANIA **1.7**

HAMBURG

BREMEN **2.0**

LOWER SAXONY **2.6**

BERLIN **1.9**

SAXONY-ANHALT **1.5**

BRANDENBURG **1.5**

NORTH RHINE-WESTPHALIA **2.6**

HESSE **2.9**

THURINGIA **1.8**

SAXONY **1.4**

RHINELAND-PALATINATE

SAARLAND **3.4**

5.9

BADEN-WÜRTTEMBERG **1.5**

BAVARIA **2.5**

Party with largest number of members *1995-96*

- CDU
- CSU
- SPD
- PDS

Source: Parteizentralen 1996

Proportion of population belonging to a party represented in the Bundestag *1995-96* percentages

- over 3%
- 2 - 3%
- below 2%

Party members *1996*

Source: Parteizentralen

Bündnis 90/Green Party	FDP	PDS	CSU	CDU	SPD
46,470	84,555	114,940	180,582	651,217	801,851

Bernhard Schäfers *The State of Germany Atlas* Copyright © Myriad Editions Limited

🌀 THE STATE AND POLITICS

Institutions to safeguard civil rights
1997
Before a formal legal battle,
committees and commissioners
represent citizens' rights.

Almost all rural and urban
districts have posts for
the protection of equal
opportunities.

In 1995, the petitions
committee of the
Bundestag received
17,067 petitions on federal
government matters.

**Referendum committees of the Bundestag
and the Landtag**
Protection of all citizens' interests.

Data protection commissioner
Maintains the rights of citizens to protect personal data
and information.

Citizens' representatives/commissioners
Defend citizens' rights on a municipal level.

Since 1994 all federal
offices with more than
200 employees have to
take on a women's
commissioner.

Women's commissioners
Defend equal opportunities for women and men.

Defence commissioner of the German Bundestag
Represents the interests of soldiers.

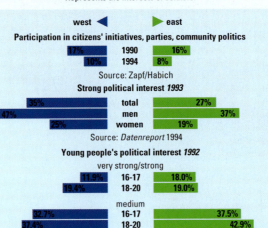

west ◄   ► east
Participation in citizens' initiatives, parties, community politics

west	year	east
17%	1990	16%
10%	1994	8%

Source: Zapf/Habich

Strong political interest *1993*

west		east
35%	total	27%
47%	men	37%
25%	women	19%

Source: *Datenreport* 1994

Young people's political interest *1992*

very strong/strong

west	age	east
11.9%	16-17	18.0%
19.4%	18-20	19.0%

medium

west	age	east
32.7%	16-17	37.5%
37.4%	18-20	42.9%

little/none

west	age	east
55.4%	16-17	44.6%
43.1%	18-20	38.1%

Source: *Das Parlament* 1993

Trust in institutions Source: infas-Repräsentativerhebung im Bundesgebiet 1995

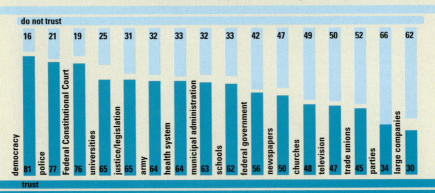

do not trust

16	21	19	25	31	32	33	32	33	42	47	49	50	52	66	62

democracy	police	Federal Constitutional Court	universities	justice/legislation	army	health system	municipal administration	schools	federal government	newspapers	churches	television	trade unions	parties	large companies
81	77	76	65	65	64	64	63	62	56	50	48	47	45	34	30

trust

Democracy depends not only on elections but on political commitment and strong systems for citizen participation.

Citizens have a new instrument of political participation in the Länder: the referendum.

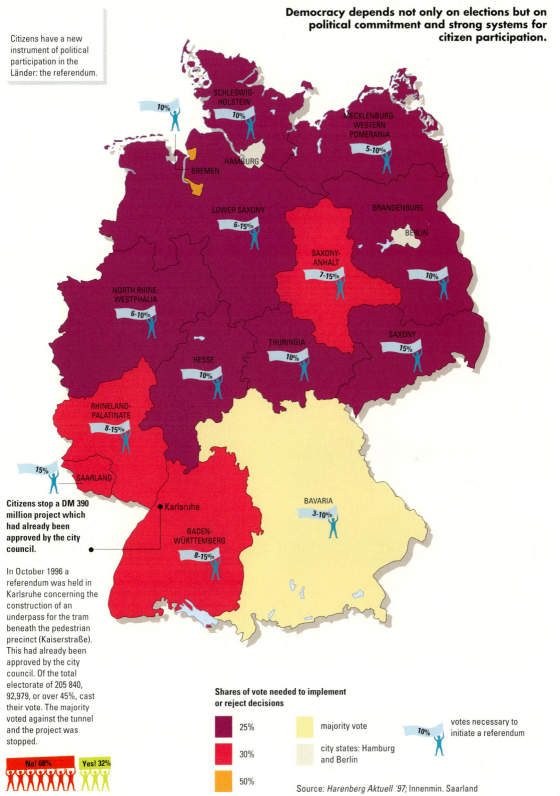

SCHLESWIG-HOLSTEIN — 10%
10%

MECKLENBURG-WESTERN POMERANIA — 5-10%

HAMBURG

BREMEN

LOWER SAXONY — 6-15%

BRANDENBURG

BERLIN

SAXONY-ANHALT — 7-15%

10%

NORTH RHINE-WESTPHALIA — 6-10%

THURINGIA — 10%

SAXONY — 15%

HESSE — 10%

RHINELAND-PALATINATE — 8-15%

15%

SAARLAND

• Karlsruhe

BAVARIA — 3-10%

BADEN-WÜRTTEMBERG — 8-15%

Citizens stop a DM 390 million project which had already been approved by the city council.

In October 1996 a referendum was held in Karlsruhe concerning the construction of an underpass for the tram beneath the pedestrian precinct (Kaiserstraße). This had already been approved by the city council. Of the total electorate of 205 840, 92,979, or over 45%, cast their vote. The majority voted against the tunnel and the project was stopped.

No! 68%   Yes! 32%

Shares of vote needed to implement or reject decisions

- 25%
- 30%
- 50%
- majority vote
- city states: Hamburg and Berlin

10% — votes necessary to initiate a referendum

Source: *Harenberg Aktuell '97*; Innenmin. Saarland

85

Resistance by the anti-nuclear movement

Across Germany, people of all age groups and social classes, including local farmers, protested against the transport of nuclear waste to the controversial intermediate storage site in the salt mines at Gorleben, Lower Saxony.

In March 1997, 800 people travelled to the site and demonstrated with the local residents against the Castor deliveries of radioactive waste from two nuclear plants in the south of Germany and the French reprocessing plant at La Hague.

The protest led to the biggest police operation in Germany's history: 30,000 police were allocated to protect the deliveries.

Intermediate storage sites *1997*

☢ intermediate storage site

☢ potential intermediate storage site

Source: Greenpeace

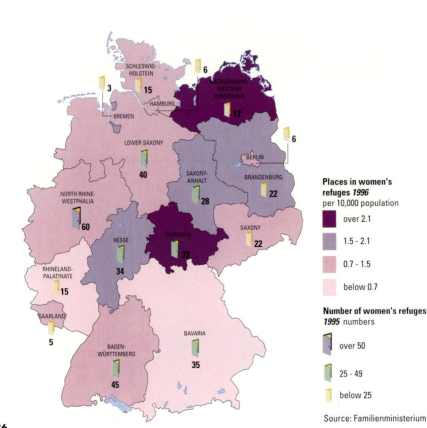

In the first year after unification, the federal government allocated DM 1.2 billion to support 47 new women's refuges.

Places in women's refuges *1996*
per 10,000 population

- over 2.1
- 1.5 - 2.1
- 0.7 - 1.5
- below 0.7

Number of women's refuges *1995* numbers

- over 50
- 25 - 49
- below 25

Source: Familienministerium

The women's movement has broken new ground by establishing refuges for abused women and children. Half the refuges are funded by independent women's groups, the remainder by welfare associations, churches and city councils.

Social movements can spring up spontaneously and react quickly. They bring together people with different backgrounds and outlooks.

The BBU (a federation of citizens' initiatives to protect the environment) was founded in 1972 by 75 initiatives with 450 members. In 1996, there were 200 initiatives, with 150,000 members.

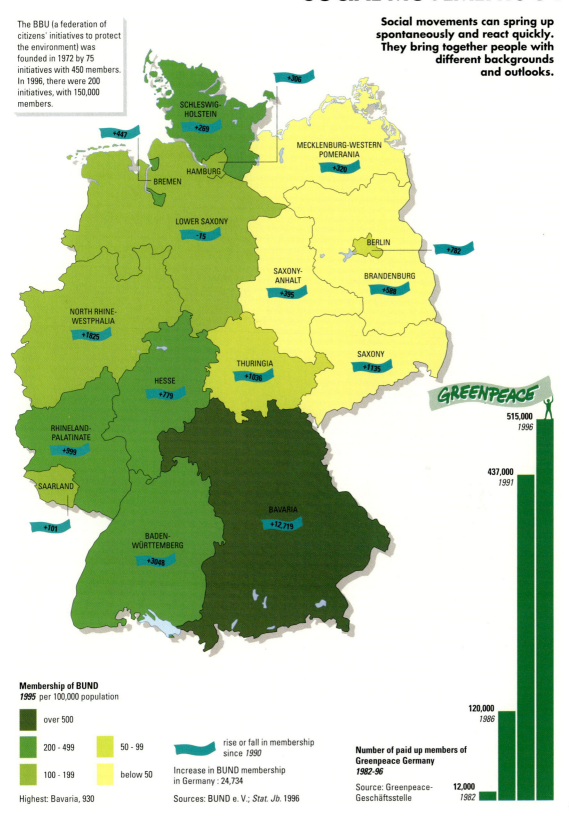

SCHLESWIG-HOLSTEIN *+306*

+269

+447

MECKLENBURG-WESTERN POMERANIA *+320*

HAMBURG

BREMEN

LOWER SAXONY *-15*

BERLIN *+782*

SAXONY-ANHALT *+395*

BRANDENBURG *+588*

NORTH RHINE-WESTPHALIA *+1825*

THURINGIA *+1036*

SAXONY *+1135*

HESSE *+779*

RHINELAND-PALATINATE *+999*

SAARLAND

+101

BAVARIA *+12,719*

BADEN-WÜRTTEMBERG *+3048*

GREENPEACE

515,000 *1996*

437,000 *1991*

120,000 *1986*

12,000 *1982*

Number of paid up members of Greenpeace Germany
1982-96

Source: Greenpeace-Geschäftsstelle

Membership of BUND
1995 per 100,000 population

- over 500
- 200 - 499
- 100 - 199
- 50 - 99
- below 50

rise or fall in membership since *1990*

Increase in BUND membership in Germany : 24,734

Highest: Bavaria, 930

Sources: BUND e. V.; *Stat. Jb.* 1996

Differences between payments from member states to the EU and from the EU to member states
1994 in DM billion

states receiving surplus

- below DM 5 billion
- over DM 5 billion

states in deficit

- below DM 5 billion
- over DM 5billion

Highest surplus: Greece, DM 7.4 billion
Highest deficit: Germany, DM 26.2 billion

Source: *Stat. Jb. Ausland* 1996

'The Euro will for the first time create the so far incorrectly titled European "single market". Prices in Europe will be transparent and comparable for the wider public for the first time.' Helmut Schmidt,

Source: *Die Zeit*

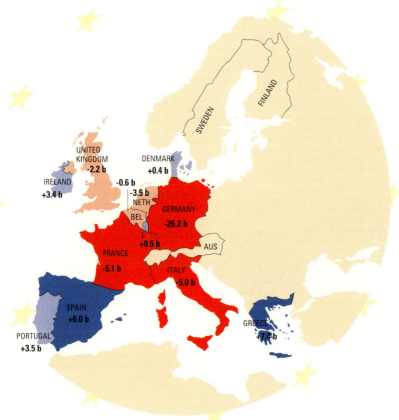

UNITED KINGDOM **-2.2 b**
IRELAND **+3.4 b**
DENMARK **+0.4 b**
-0.6 b
-3.5 b
NETH
BEL
GERMANY **-26.2 b**
L **+0.5 b**
AUS
FRANCE **-5.1 b**
ITALY **-5.0 b**
SPAIN **+6.0 b**
PORTUGAL **+3.5 b**
GREECE **-7.4 b**

Inflation below 2.9%

Finland 1.0%	met	
Germany 1.6%	met	
Luxembourg 1.7%	met	
Sweden 1.7%	met	
Denmark 1.8%	met	
France 1.8%	met	
Netherlands 1.9%	met	
Belgium 2.0%	met	
Austria 2.1%	met	
Ireland 2.3%	met	
UK 2.7%	met	
Portugal 3.1%	not met	
Spain 3.6%	not met	
Italy 4.1%	not met	
Greece 8.3%	not met	

Budget deficit

Luxembourg 0.7%	met	
Denmark -0.9%	met	
Ireland -2.0%	met	
Belgium -3.2%	not met	
Finland -3.3%	not met	
Netherlands -3.5%	not met	
Germany -3.9%	not met	
France -4.2%	not met	
UK -4.4%	not met	
Portugal -4.4%	not met	
Austria -4.6%	not met	
Spain -4.8%	not met	
Sweden -5.2%	not met	
Italy -6.3%	not met	
Greece -8.1%	not met	

Government debt

Luxembourg 6.2%	met	
UK 55.5%	met	
France 56.1%	met	
Germany 61.5%	not met	
Finland 62.5%	not met	
Spain 67.8%	not met	
Denmark 71.0%	not met	
Portugal 72.2%	not met	
Austria 72.4%	not met	
Netherlands 79.4%	not met	
Sweden 80.8%	not met	
Ireland 81.3%	not met	
Greece 111.8%	not met	
Italy 124.5%	not met	
Belgium 132.2%	not met	

Survey on EMU *1996*

58% of the population: against
83% of managers: in favour.

Source: *Allensbacher Archiv*

Fit for EMU? How countries met the Maastricht criteria *1996*

Inflation below 2.9%
- met
- not met

Budget deficit less than 3% of GDP
- met
- not met

Government debt less than 60% of GDP
- met
- not met

Source: Globus 1996

Until 2002, the EU currency unit is the Ecu, or European Currency Unit. 1 Ecu =1.93 DM (November 1996). The Euro replaces the Ecu in 2002.

After two disastrous world wars, Europe unites wide range of economies and democracies.

European Union
1996

members since

- founding member of European Coal and Steel Community 1951, and later the European Economic Community and European Atomic Energy Community (Euratom), 1957
- first expansion of European Community 1973
- second expansion 1983
- third expansion 1986
- fourth expansion, European Union, 1995

- membership applied for
- associate member
- associate membership sought

- ■ seat of European institution
- ■ European Cities of Culture (elected by the EU for one year, since 1985)

Source: Globus

- The Committee of the Regions consists of 222 representatives of states, regions and municipalities. Germany has 24 delegates (21 Länder/regional representatives and 3 municipal ones).

- The Committee is to be consulted, for example, on educational funding, cultural funding, trans-European networks, structural and regional policy.

German-speaking Spanish	Spanish-speaking Germans	German-speaking Italians	Italian-speaking Germans	German-speaking French	French-speaking Germans	German-speaking British	English-speaking Germans
1%	4%	4%	3%	9%	16%	9%	44%

Adults with knowledge of foreign languages *1991*
percentages of population

Source: Spiegel-Dokumentation 1993

THE LÄNDER IN FIGURES

	1 Population 1995 in 1000	2 Land area km²	3 Population per km² 1995 	Built up area 1993 percent	4 Traffic area 1993 percent	Forest 1993 percent
Baden-Württemberg	10,296	35,751	288	6.3	5.2	37.7
Bavaria	11,952	70,547	169	4.3	4.1	34.2
Berlin	3470	889	3470	42.7	12.4	17.4
Brandenburg	2536	29,481	86	3.7	3.3	34.7
Bremen	680	404	1682	32.7	11.9	2.0
Hamburg	1707	755	2260	34.4	11.7	4.5
Hesse	5993	21,114	284	6.7	6.5	39.8
Lower Saxony	7745	47,606	163	6.1	4.8	20.8
Mecklenburg-Western Pomerania	1829	23,169	79	3.1	2.5	21.2
North Rhine-Westphalia	17,839	34,072	524	11.3	6.4	24.7
Rhineland-Palatinate	3962	19,845	200	4.9	5.9	40.5
Saarland	1083	2570	421	11.2	6.0	33.4
Saxony	4575	18,409	249	5.6	3.6	26.4
Saxony-Anhalt	2750	20,446	135	4.0	3.5	21.2
Schleswig-Holstein	2716	15,739	173	5.5	4.0	9.2
Thuringia	2511	16,175	155	3.7	3.8	31.8
Germany	**81,643**	**356,974**	**229**	**5.8**	**4.6**	**29.2**

	9 Gross domestic product (GDP)			10 Voter participation		
	1996 million DM provisional	1995 1000 DM per person	1995 1000 DM per person in workforce	1994 13th German Bundestag percent	latest Landtag elections percent	1994 European Parliament elections percent
Baden-Württemberg	509.6	48.0	106.1	79.7	67.6	66.4
Bavaria	596.0	48.7	106.1	76.9	67.8	56.4
Berlin	149.9	42.6	97.7	78.6	68.6	53.5
Brandenburg	67.8	25.2	52.3	71.5	56.3	41.5
Bremen	39.3	58.4	113.5	78.5	68.6	52.7
Hamburg	136.6	78.7	147.5	79.7	69.6	51.7
Hesse	343.4	56.8	129.8	82.3	66.3	56.4
Lower Saxony	315.4	39.6	98.4	81.8	73.8	52.7
Mecklenburg-Western Pomerania	44.5	22.6	54.1	72.8	72.9	65.8
North Rhine-Westphalia	787.7	43.2	108.4	81.9	64.0	59.5
Rhineland Palatinate	150.1	38.3	102.3	82.3	70.8	74.3
Saarland	43.9	39.6	97.2	83.5	83.5	74.1
Saxony	116.5	23.9	56.1	72.0	58.4	70.2
Saxony-Anhalt	66.1	23.7	57.7	70.4	54.8	66.1
Schleswig-Holstein	110.9	40.4	100.6	80.9	71.8	51.3
Thuringia	61.0	23.5	57.1	74.9	74.8	71.9
Germany	**3539**	**42.4**	**99.2**	**79.0**	**–**	**60.0**

Sources: **columns 1 and 2:** *Zahlen 1996;* **columns 3 and 4:** *Stat. Jb.1995, 1996;* **column 5**: *Globus 3990/1997; Zahlen 1996;*
column 6: *Stat. Jb. 1996*

	5 Population in municipalities 1993 over 100,000 people, percent	6 Spending on higher education 1993 per person DM	7 School leavers: Gymnasium/ secondary school 1994 per 1000 population	girls percent	8 Share of workforce in manufacturing 1995 per 1000 population
Baden-Württemberg	19.4	600	2.2	51.9	124
Bavaria	21.8	532	1.8	51.0	103
Berlin	100.0	1278	2.4	54.4	44
Brandenburg	10.5	134	no data	no data	39
Bremen	100.0	580	2.9	51.9	103
Hamburg	100.0	1000	2.9	51.7	69
Hesse	23.3	560	2.5	52.1	88
Lower Saxony	20.7	451	2.3	60.9	27
Mecklenburg-Western Pomerania	19.5	476	3.0	52.5	92
North Rhine-Westphalia	47.5	493	2.6	52.6	74
Rhineland-Palatinate	14.4	419	2.2	52.8	82
Saarland	17.6	773	1.9	51.2	104
Saxony	29.4	531	2.4	61.0	46
Saxony-Anhalt	20.4	481	2.8	60.2	44
Schleswig-Holstein	17.3	524	2.0	50.6	56
Thuringia	16.7	509	2.7	60.7	44
Germany	**32.0**	**521**	**2.3**	**53.6**	**83**

Federal offices (selected)

Baden-Württemberg	**Karlsruhe**: Bundesverfassungsgericht, Bundesgerichtshof, Bundesamt für Wasserbau, Bundesforschungsanstalt für Ernährung
Bavaria	**Munich**: Bundesfinanzhof, Bundespatentamt; **Pullach bei München**: Bundesnachrichtendienst; **Nuremberg**: Bundesanstalt für Arbeit
Berlin	Amtssitz des Bundespräsidenten, Bundesverwaltungsgericht, Bundeskartellamt, Bundesaufsichtsamt für das Kreditwesen, Bundesaufsichtsamt für das Versicherungswesen, Bundesinstitut für Berufsbildung, Umweltbundesamt, Bundesversicherungsamt, Bundesgesundheitsamt, Bundesbaubehörde
Hamburg	Bundesamt für Seeschiffahrt, Bundesforschungsanstalt für Fischerei
Hesse	**Frankfurt**: Bundesrechnungshof, Bundesamt für Ernährung und Forstwirtschaft, Bundesamt für Wirtschaft, Deutsche Bundesbahn, Deutsche Bundesbank, Deutsche Bibliothek; **Kassel**: Bundesarbeitsgericht, Bundessozialgericht; **Offenbach**: Bundesanstalt für Flugsicherung, Deutscher Wetterdienst; **Wiesbaden**: Statistisches Bundesamt, Bundeskriminalamt
Lower Saxony	**Braunschweig**: Luftfahrt-Bundesamt, Physikalisch-Technische Bundesanstalt; **Hanover**: Bundesanstalt für Geowissenschaften und Rohstoffe; **Salzgitter**: Bundesamt für Strahlenschutz
North Rhine-Westphalia	**Bergisch-Gladbach**: Bundesanstalt für Straßenwesen; **Bonn**: (still) Sitz aller Bundesministerien/des Bundesrates, Bundeszentrale für politische Bildung, Bundesforschungsanstalt für Landeskunde und Raumordnung, Deutsche Bundespost; **Dortmund**: Bundesanstalt für Arbeitsschutz; **Cologne**: Bundesamt für Verfassungsschutz, Militärischer Abschirmdienst, Bundesinstitut für Sportwissenschaft
Rhineland-Palatinate	**Koblenz**: Bundesarchiv, Bundesamt für Wehrtechnik und Beschaffung, Bundesamt für Gewässerkunde
Saxony	**Leipzig**: Deutsche Bibliothek (second location)
Schleswig-Holstein	**Flensburg**: Kraftfahrt-Bundesamt; **Kiel**: Bundesanstalt für Milchforschung
Thuringia	**Erfurt** (from 2000): Bundesarbeitsgericht (from Kassel)

Sources: column 7: *Stat. Jb.* 1996; **columns 8 and 9:** *Stat. Jb.* 1996; **column 10:** *Zahlen*1996;
Federal offices: *Jb. der Br.* 1996

COMMENTARY

1 THE POPULATION

After the Second World War, in 1949, two separate German states were set up: the Federal Republic of Germany (FRG or West Germany) and the German Democratic Republic (GDR or East Germany). On 3 October 1990, they united to form a new Federal Republic of Germany. Five new Länder (states) were established out of the old GDR. East Berlin, which had also been part of the GDR, was amalgamated with West Berlin as a *Stadtstaat* (city state). The eight Länder and two *Stadtstaaten* (Hamburg and Bremen) of former West Germany are frequently referred to as the 'old' Länder. The population is not very evenly distributed across the country.

Between 1949 and 1989 the East German population fell by 2.7 million, down to a total of 16.6 million, most of whom moved into West Germany. The border between the two countries was hermetically sealed with the building of the Berlin Wall in August 1961 (see also **6. Mobility**). As many as several hundred people may have died trying to cross the wall to West Berlin and the whole frontier between East and West Germany became known as the 'death strips'. Despite this, East Germany failed to check the decline in its population. The birth rate also sank so low that for some years it was the lowest in the world.

As in many other countries, the growth of an industrial middle class and major improvements in social hygiene and medicine have meant a continual rise in life expectancy from the mid 19th century. Life expectancy for women born 1871-80 was only 48.1 years and for men 46.5 years.

The generation ratio compares the number of girls born to the number of women aged 15 to 50, their reproductive years. In West Germany in 1965 the ratio was 1.17 girls born for every woman aged 15 to 50. By 1987 the ratio had dropped to 0.64:1. This means that only 64 percent of the mother's generation was being substituted by daughters.

The gender ratio refers to the distribution of births between boys and girls. In all western industrialized nations about 105 boys are born for every 100 girls, which is an an imbalance. Over the years, however, this is virtually reversed. The overall gender ratio is 100 men for every 103 women. Infant mortality is higher in male children, as are the accident and suicide rates of young men, but the main cause is that women tend to live longer than men.

In some developing countries, children below 15 years old make up roughly half the population. In industrial countries this proportion has fallen dramatically, and in Germany it is now down to 16.4 percent. Meanwhile the proportion of people over 65 has risen strongly. This shift affects families, and society as a whole. It affects kindergartens, the education system and employment in general. It is one of the biggest factors affecting the welfare state, in particular old age pensions.

This trend cuts right across the European Union (EU). Population statisticians say that on average women need to produce 2.15 children to maintain a stable population. In 1990, Ireland was the only EU country to achieve this. Elsewhere birth rates were markedly lower. In Italy the rate was 1.31, the lowest in the EU. The rate in France was 1.78, and in the UK 1.84, both being higher than the EU average of 1.59. Women in the EU had 25 percent fewer children than was necessary to maintain the current population. The fact that the population of former West Germany, and later Germany as a whole, has continued to rise is due only to immigration.

Sources: R. Geißler, T. Meyer, Struktur und Entwicklung der Bevölkerung, in: R. Geißler, Die Sozialstruktur Deutschlands, 2. Aufl., Opladen 1996, S. 333-357; P. Marschalck, Bevölkerungsgeschichte Deutschlands im 19. und 20. Jh., Frankfurt a. M. 1984; B. Schäfers, Bevölkerungsstruktur. Wanderungen, in: ders., 1995 (vgl. S. 8), S. 88-110.

2 HOUSEHOLDS

In socioeconomic terms, households are units in which people, not necessarily related, live together and share domestic financial arrangements. In sociobiological terms, the family is a unit mainly characterized by the relationship between parents and children. The term 'lifestyle' can be used to describe the ways in which people live together, or the social structure of the population.

Since the nineteenth century rapid changes have been taking place in all industrial societies. In general the size of both households and families has been going down, while the range of individual lifestyles has become broader. Far fewer households are now based on families of two or more generations, and the number of single person households is rising rapidly.

These changes are an expression of social and cultural change and reflect how people are adapting to the changing age structure of the population (see **1. Population**), as well as changes in education, work and ways of life. Society has become more geared to individual needs. Lifestyles are more diverse as people redefine their social positions and roles (with regard to parenthood, for example) according to their personal ideas and values. The social position of women is changing as they search for careers and financial independence.

There are many new ways of sharing a household. There are more single parent families and many couples now live in two households, in the same or different locations. Today's partners cannot always find jobs in the same city, and when a man moves because of his job, it can no longer be guaranteed that his partner will give up her own job to follow him. Lifestyles can change greatly with age. Small numbers of children per family and longer life expectancy mean that the family phase represents about a quarter of total lifespan. The large increase in single person households reflects an urge for personal flexibility. This is especially true for the many single people who choose to live by themselves but still maintain a relationship.

The big gap between the number of single person households in the old and new Länder can be explained by East Germany's family centred housing policy. In the east, most single person households are occupied by old people, especially women. The high proportion of single person households – about 35 percent of the total – should not be interpreted as a loss of community. Nor should the increasing number of divorces. Many divorcees remarry or go on to live with new partners. Since the early 1970s, a new group culture has begun to emerge and new social and cooperative networks are being added to traditional families and households of blood relatives.

Sources: W. Glatzer, Haushalte und Haushaltsproduktionen, in: Handwörterbuch zur Gesellschaft Deutschlands, hg. v. B. Schäfers u. W. Zapf, Opladen 1997; R. Peuckert, Familienformen im Wandel, 2. Aufl., Opladen 1996; Datenreport 1994, S.31f.

3 TOWN AND COUNTRY

With the exception of Russia, Germany is the most highly populated country in Europe. At 222 people per square kilometre, its population density is only exceeded by the Netherlands, Belgium and the UK. In the old Länder there are 259 people per sqare kilometre, in the new Länder, 146.

There are a few very sparsely populated areas, as in Mecklenburg-Western Pomerania (Mecklenburg-Vorpommern) or Saxony-Anhalt (Sachsen-Anhalt), but almost none of the empty spaces to be found in France, Italy, or Spain. There are large cities and conurbations, but no straggling urban agglomerations such as Paris or Athens. The Rhine-Ruhr is less an urban agglomeration than a series of individual cities linked together.

Thirty two percent of Germany's 82 million people live in its megacities plus 70 other large cities. Berlin has a population of 3.5 million, Hamburg 1.7 million, Munich (München) 1.3 million, Cologne (Köln) nearly a million. Twenty six percent live in medium sized cities of 20,000-100,000; 24 percent in small towns of 5000-20,000, and 18 percent in small rural towns and municipalities. Since the major reorganization of the municipalities (*Gemeinden*) between 1968 and 1975 , 53 percent live in conurbations (such as Berlin, Hamburg, the Rhine-Ruhr, Rhine-Main, Rhine-Neckar, Halle-Leipzig and Stuttgart), 30 percent live in urban areas and 17 percent in rural areas.

Germans identify strongly with their cities. This is why the autonomy of the municipalities – embedded in German history and acknowledged in the Basic Law – is so central to social life. It is rightly acknowledged that the *genius loci* of East Germany's historically and culturally important but neglected cities made rapid change possible after unification. The spirit of Weimar, Potsdam, Dresden and Leipzig, Halle and Rostock rose up and created building blocks for unification. Coming from Berlin, Dresden or Hamburg always has greater meaning than being a mere resident. This sense of identity is even stronger in the old towns or small cities. Many towns such as Detmold or Baden-Baden have their own independent theatre. All have their own schools and colleges, sports facilities and town hall. They may often have a well-established university (as do Marburg and Tübingen) or a newer technical college.

Some cities are more controversial: especially those grown onto the edge of other cities, large-scale accommodation facilities built in the 1960s and 1970s and colloquially known as dormitories (*Schlafstädte)* or 'test-tube' cities (*Retortenstädte*). These have come into being largely because they offer a comfortable standard of living, including bathrooms and own toilets, not hitherto enjoyed by many families. They were widely welcomed in East Germany since urban housing was in a very poor state and did not benefit from the renovation and modernization of West German housing that went on in the 1950s and 1960s.

From the 1960s onwards, West Germany's inner cities became service areas, which led to a huge increase in city centre traffic. Those who were able, especially young families with children, moved out to the rapidly growing suburbs.

In spite of a heavy degree of urbanization, Germany's agricultural and forest lands are almost as large as they were at the beginning of the industrial age.

Sources: Bundesforschungsanstalt für Landeskunde und Raumordnung, Mitteilungen und Informationen 2/96; Raumordnungsbericht der Bundesregierung, Bonn 1993; B. Schäfers u. G. Wewer, Hg., Die Stadt in Deutschland, Opladen 1996.

4 HOME

Housing quality is a good indicator of how people feel about life in general. In the history of both West and East Germany, the need to provide affordable and well built housing has been central to the success of the social market economy and social policy.

In West Germany, between 1951 and 1960, council housing represented 55 percent of the total housing market; in the 1970s this sank to 37 percent and during the 1980s it fell further, to 20 percent. There was a steep increase, however, in the size of flats. In 1950, after the first phase of reconstruction in the three western zones, living space per person was 14.3 square metres, but only 62 percent of households had a flat to themselves. After the Second World War, there were large numbers of refugees from the east to be accommodated and many towns and cities had been destroyed. But by 1970, living space per person had risen to 23.8 square metres. In the late 1990s, German households have about 39 square metres per person and non German households 21 square metres. On average, one person households have 55 square metres, two person households, 36, and four person households only 23.

Rent on its own is a large part of household living expenses, but utility bills have now risen to the point where they are virtually a second rent. In the west there are special charges for rubbish collection which have almost doubled. In the east the cost of chimney sweeps, which are still used, has recently trebled.

For historical reasons, there is a big difference in housing between west and east. No other socialist state was as dogmatic on the question of home ownership as East Germany. In 1950, 61 percent of East German homes were owned, but by 1968 this figure was down to 5 percent, lower than anywhere else in Europe. By the end of 1993, living space per person was 29.3 square metres in the east compared with 36.9 square metres in the west. Only half of all homes in the east had bathrooms, toilets and central heating, compared with about 80 percent in the west.

Most Germans would like to live in a quiet and pleasant area and own their own home. But home ownership figures in Germany are much lower than elsewhere in Europe. The costs of accommodation and building are both comparatively high, partly due to the high cost of land and rigid building regulations.

Traditionally families have always tried to extend their living space. In the nineteenth century, Daniel Schreber (1808-61) a Leipzig doctor, established a movement to promote garden allotments (*Schrebergarten*) to counteract the cramped and unhealthy living conditions of the cities. Such allotments are often very large and like so much else in Germany, tend to be organized by a community association or *Verein* (see **16. Clubs and Associations**). They are usually well kept and furnished with a small but comfortable hut or cabin. They are very popular for family gatherings, barbecues and so on. In former East Germany, where living conditions and the political climate were harder, these allotments, including little weekend homes (*Datschen*), were probably thought to be even more valuable. They provided extra living space, free from external control, where personal belongings could be swapped or repaired.

Many Germans have second or holiday homes, which may be in Germany, Europe (in Tuscany, the south of France or Mallorca for example), or as far afield as Florida.

Sources: Gesamtverband der Wohnungswirtschaft e. V., Hg., Schrift Nr. 37: Wohnungseigentum in Deutschland, Köln 1992; H. Häußermann u. W. Siebel, Soziologie des Wohnens, Weinheim, München 1996; Informationen zur Raumentwicklung der Bundesforschungsanstalt für Landeskunde und Raumordnung, verschied. Hefte; Raumordnungsprognose 2010 der Bundesforschungsanstalt für Landeskunde und Raumordnung, Bonn 1995; Statistisches Bundesamt, Hg., Fachserie 5 / Reihe 3: Bautätigkeit und Wohnungen; Globus Nr. 3948/1997; Mikrozensus 1993.

5 THE ENVIRONMENT

The environmental movement began in the late 1960s and made a rapid impact, especially in West Germany. The first UN conference on the environment was held in Stockholm in 1971. In 1972-73, the so-called oil crisis drew attention to the finite nature of many natural resources. A new vocabulary came into common usage, such as chlorofluorocarbons (CFCs), carbon dioxide, ecology, and the hole in the ozone layer.

In 1972 a UN report, *The Limits of Growth* stated: 'If the current increase in the world's population, industrialization, environmental pollution, food production and exploitation of natural resources remain unchanged, the absolute limits of growth on this earth will be reached within the next 100 years.' Twenty years later, in the *The New Limits of Growth*, the same authors expressed stronger concerns, arguing that the use of many natural resources and the release of many harmful substances that decompose only with difficulty have already passed the limit of what is physically possible over an even longer period of time. Environmental problems can be solved only by national commitment and international cooperation. The use of CFCs and fossil fuel emissions are not merely private or national questions. They endanger all living beings.

In Germany, the need for technology and the economy to be environmentally friendly has long been a major concern. There has also been a change in conscience and attitudes since the 1970s. After the federal government's first environmental programme was announced in 1971, new environmental protection laws were ratified. In 1974, the Federal Office for the Environment (UBA or *Umweltbundesamt*) was set up. Its responsibilities include public education on environmental issues and the improvement of information systems on environmental damage. Immediately after the nuclear reactor accident at Chernobyl in April 1986 a new body was set up: the Federal Ministry for the Environment, Protection of Nature and Reactor Safety.

The term 'old damage' refers to problems decades or even a century old: for example traces in the soil from former industrial areas or damage caused by former German and foreign military units (*Rüstungsaltlasten*).

In 1993, OECD data showed that Germany's strong environmental controls had paid off. It was doing better than any other industrial nation in controlling air pollution, dealing with waste and protecting its inland waters. But there is no room for complacency. The Red List of the Federal Office for the Protection of Nature has estimated that more than two thirds of a total of 509 natural habitats are endangered, including almost all those most significant. Although the death of German forests can be slowed, large parts of forest cover are still in danger.

Since the 1992 UN summit on the environment and development in Rio de Janeiro, the term 'sustainable development' has become a catchword in ecology, and in economic and environmental policy. Since then all plans for the development of the economy, cities, regions or transport should in theory provide for the maintenance and renewal of natural resources. But neither the Rio summit nor the 1995 world climate conference in Berlin achieved an effective degree of protection.

Opposition to the notion of sustainable development stems from the economic interests of industrial as well as developing countries. The former export many of their environmental problems, the latter 'profit' from non-existent regulations by producing cheap manufactured goods for the rich world.

Sources: Bundestagsdrucksachen 12/8451, 13/4108, 13/4767, 13/4825, 13/5146, Bonn 1996; B. Hamm u. I. Neumann, Siedlungs-, Umwelt- und Planungssoziologie. Ökologische Soz. Bd. 2, Opladen 1996; D. H. Meadows u. a., Die Grenzen des Wachstums, Stuttgart 1992 (1972); Dies., Die neuen Grenzen des Wachstums, Stuttgart 1992; Joni Seager, Der Öko-Atlas, 2. Aufl. Neuausgabe, Bonn 1997; Umweltbundesamt, Hg., Was Sie schon immer über Abfall und Umwelt wissen wollten, 3. Aufl., Stuttgart u. a. 1993.

6 MOBILITY

Horizontal mobility refers to those who move home – to another municipality (*Gemeinde*), Land, or even abroad. Such mobility can be further divided into internal and external mobility.

There is much more mobility in Germany than one might expect. If moves within municipalities are included, German society is clearly in a constant state of flux. In Karlsruhe, for example, a city with a population of 269,000, some 23,000 (8.6 percent) moved home in 1995 alone. However mobility between municipalities has limited value as an indicator. In a major reorganization between 1968 and 1975, 24,282 municipalities in West Germany were reduced to 8502, or by two thirds.

In the post war period and early years of the new West German Federal Republic, most mobility was the result of flight and expulsions. Before April 1947, 10.1 million German settlers were sent back from Eastern Europe into West Germany as *Zwangsaussiedler*. Until 1961, when the Berlin Wall was built and the border tightly sealed, the socialist regime created a further stream of refugees to the West. From then on, the level of east-west mobility was determined by the policy of the East German regime. On the whole there was little or no movement except for a short period in the mid 1980s, when the East German government temporarily relented and issued large numbers of exit visas.

Voluntary mobility was impossible until November 1989 when the Berlin Wall came down. In July 1990, an economic, social and currency union was set up between the two German states. This union preceded unification itself in October 1990 and its main purpose was to contain a rush of potential migrants from east to west.

People also move home, of course, for personal and family reasons. Indeed migration could be described as a part of problem solving social behaviour. It is a response to changing family size, or a need for different living conditions, working conditions or educational opportunities. Local mobility can also be used to signal a change of social status. Mobility between countries is often job related and for a fixed period of time.

Fewer people are now moving to change their geographical location and more people are moving for work reasons. All forms of weekend and leisure time mobility are steadily increasing.

Sources: Deutschland-Archiv 22(1989) und 24 (1991); S. Grundmann, Die Ost-West-Wanderung in Deutschland (1989-1992), in: H. Bertram u. a., Hg., Sozialer und demographischer Wandel in den neuen Bundesländern, Berlin 1995; W. Weidenfeld und H. Zimmermann, Hg., Deutschland-Handbuch. Eine doppelte Bilanz 1949-1989, Bonn 1989.

7 IMMIGRATION

Is Germany an 'immigration country'? This question is deeply controversial. The federal government asserts that Germany is not an immigration country and that it has no immigration quota policy and no plans, for example, to introduce a US style green card system. Yet studies of mobility in Germany over the last hundred years show that no other country in Europe has experienced such continually high levels of immigration.

Before 1961, when the Berlin Wall was built and East Germany closed off, most immigration into West Germany was European. This was partly the result of industrialization and urbanization, but mainly the result of the devastation caused by two world wars. Since then immigration into Germany, and also the rest of Europe, has had a multicultural face. In the 1960s, the Italians were the largest immigrant group. Since the early 1970s, Turkish workers and their families have not only been the largest immigrant group, they have also become the largest non Christian religious group in Germany. Like other immigrant workers arriving in Europe, they were enticed with job contracts and were a source of cheap labour.

Asylum seekers are people who seek refuge abroad on grounds of political, ethnic or religious persecution at home. They are for the most part a reflection of the world's wars, civil wars and natural disasters. The number of asylum seekers has soared since the 1970s and in 1992 alone there were 438,000 in Germany. Until 1993, Germany had one of the most liberal asylum laws in the world, but this was then curtailed by constitutional amendment and integrated into the Basic Law. Although the article still maintains the principle that 'Those who are politically persecuted should enjoy the right to asylum', paragraphs 2 to 4 contain clear limitations. The amendment had an immediate impact. While Germany received some 322,000 applications for asylum in 1993, the number fell sharply to 63,000 in the first six months of 1994. The rate of acceptance of asylum seekers is low: in 1995 it was 5 percent.

Aussiedler (ethnic Germans) are German according to the Basic Law, but have not lived in Germany for a generation or more. In 1988, 203,000 ethnic Germans arrived in Germany who were foreigners by country of origin, but German by ethnic origin. They included 140,000 from Poland and 48,000 from the (then) USSR. Between 1962 and 1993, Germany accepted as many as 2.6 million ethnic Germans, but since 1996 the numbers have been cut back. In future they will have to offer more detailed proof of their German roots. The Basic Law now states that German citizenship will be given to those who have adhered in their home environment to the German ethnic tradition, which should be confirmed by certain traits such as origin, language, education, or culture. In addition to the Basic Law, the Länder have agreed that all people are German who can prove that they or their ancestors have been treated as German since 1 January 1914. Being born in Germany does not give one the right to be a German citizen.

Refugees must also be counted as immigrants, though they may be temporary ones. Up to March 1995, Germany accepted 350,000 refugees from the wars in former Yugoslavia. These refugees will only gradually return to their home countries.

In 1995, there were more than seven million foreigners in Germany, or 8.8 percent of the total population. This figure includes two million Turkish people. The current restrictions of Germany's citizenship law need urgent review. As the countries of Europe move closer together, they need to live harmoniously with each other and with their neighbours in North Africa and the Middle East.

Sources: Beauftragte der Bundesregierung f. d. Belange d. Ausländer, Hg., Bericht über die Lage der Ausländer in der Bundesrepublik Deutschland, Bonn 1995; K.-H. Meier-Braun: 40 Jahre „Gastarbeiter" und Ausländerpolitik in Deutschland, in: Beilage zur Wochenzeitung DAS PARLAMENT v. 25.8.1995 u. v. 25.10.1996; C. Schmalz-Jacobsen u. G. Hansen, Hg., Ethnische Minderheiten in der BRD. Ein Lexikon, München 1995; Senatsverwaltung f. Stadtentwicklung, Umweltschutz und Technologie, Hg., Migration in Berlin: Zuwanderung, gesellschaftliche Probleme, politische Ansätze, Berlin 1995; Der Spiegel 16/1997; Bundestagsdrucksache v. 18.3.1997.

8 SOCIAL CLASS AND MILIEUS

Incomes and wealth, property ownership and education, professional position and other fundamentals of life and living together are very unevenly distributed in Germany. Social class describes social and economic status. Milieus describe cultural attitudes and lifestyles.

There are in principle three responses to social inequality. It can be seen as given by nature or God (as in medieval society) and therefore accepted unquestioningly. It can be seen as an encumbrance to a strongly unified society (as in all socialist utopias) and rejected entirely. Or it can be accepted within certain limits. Like the rest of the Western world, Germany's response is the latter.

As long as whole groups of people are not excluded (for example, the long term unemployed), social inequality is tolerated as an expression of individual needs for education and success. Article 15 of the Basic Law stipulates that property owning bears a social duty, and that taxation and the social state are a means of creating an egalitarian society. Nevertheless Germany, like other Western democracies, has only partially realized this principle of social equality (along with liberty and fraternity, one of the fundamentals of a modern egalitarian society). Former East Germany succeeded somewhat better, but paid a high price.

Germans have a strong sense of social position. In an imaginary class pyramid, divided into the traditional upper, middle and lower classes, their subjective judgements are close to objective ones.

New movements, new lifestyles, changes in employment and the growth of long term unemployment have all led to dramatic changes in traditional class since the late 1970s. Research on social inequality identifies a growing emphasis on the individual and a greater range of accepted lifestyles. It also reports that the lifestyles of traditional industrial societies are declining in influence. Subcultures are tending to develop which are increasingly distant from the traditional forms of the middle class family. Youth cultures and alternative social scenes are to be found in the major cities such as Berlin or Hamburg, or in university towns such as Göttingen and Freiburg.

There has also been a growth of ethnic communities in second or third generation immigrants and the rest of the non German population.

With the unification of Germany in 1990, a basically classless, egalitarian workers' society became exposed to the complex social milieus of the West.

High and long term unemployment, the integration problems of ethnic Germans, and cutbacks in the welfare state have moved Germany towards being a 'two-thirds society'. This is a society where two thirds of the population have a job and secure pension and belong to the 'normal' population; and where one third is marginalized – economically, socially, culturally, and ultimately politically, cut off.

Sources:. Beck, Risikogesellschaft, Frankfurt 1986; M. Diewald u. A. Sørensen, Erwerbsverläufe und soziale Mobilität von Frauen und Männern in Ostdeutschland, in: M. Diewald u. K. U. Mayer, Hg., Zwischenbilanz der Wiedervereinigung, Opladen 1996; St. Hradil, Sozialstruktur in einer fortgeschrittenen Gesellschaft. Von Klassen und Schichten zu Lagen und Milieus, Opladen 1987; H.-H. Noll, Ungleichheit der Lebenslagen und ihre Legitimation im Transformationsprozeß: Fakten, Perzeptionen und Bewertungen, in: L. Clausen, Hg., Gesellschaften im Umbruch, Frankfurt a. M., New York 1996; G. Schulze, Die Erlebnisgesellschaft, 4. Aufl., Frankfurt a. M., New York 1993; R. Geißler, Die Sozialstruktur Deutschlands, 2. erw. Aufl., Opladen 1996.

9 RICH AND POOR

Poverty in Germany is mainly perceived as financial poverty. Disposable net income per household is the key indicator that shows when households fall below the minimum income required for survival (the poverty threshold) or below the ceiling which triggers income support.

In the 1960s, unemployment was sometimes below 1 percent and poverty was almost a forgotten concept. In the 1970s, though at first sporadic and half hidden, poverty returned to the streets and homelessness increased dramatically. In West Germany the proportion on income support rose from 1.3 percent in 1963 to 4.7 percent in 1992. If by poverty we mean having less than 50 percent of average net income, in 1992, 6.3 million or 7.8 percent of all households in Germany should be described as poor: in old Länder 6.5 percent, in the new, 12.7 percent.

Before state pensions improved in the 1970s, the poor were mainly older, single people and were primarily women. Today's poor are the long term unemployed, single mothers and large numbers of foreigners. Between 1963 and 1992, the rate of income support for 17 year olds rose from 1.7 percent to 8.7 percent, and for 18 to 24 year olds from 0.5 percent to 6.2 percent. More families with children are now at risk. There has also been a rise in the number living in long term poverty. From a number of studies, G. E. Zimmermann concludes that at least 2 million people (almost 3 percent of the population) have suffered from long term poverty for over five years.

Since the 1970s, poverty has also been increasing in the European Union. The first European Community programme on fighting poverty in member states covered the period 1975-81.

Riches are mainly defined by wealth rather than income. By wealth we mean money, property, bonds, shares, savings, insurance and capital wealth. The distribution of wealth is much more unequal than the distribution of incomes. Few households can claim a large share of the country's total wealth.

The uneven distribution of income between households and families is clear. The bottom 20 percent in east Germany have a third of the income of the top 20 percent; in the west they have only a quarter.

Sources:. S. Dangschat, „Stadt" als Ort und Ursache von Armut und sozialer Ausgrenzung, in: Beilage zur Zeitschrift DAS PARLAMENT 31-32/1995; R. Geißler, Die Sozialstruktur Deutschlands, Opladen 1996; W. Glatzer u. H.-H. Noll, Getrennt vereint: Lebensverhältnisse in Deutschland seit der Wiedervereinigung, Frankfurt a. M., New York 1995; Globus in: Süddeutsche Zeitung v. 11.12.1996; R. Hauser, Das empirische Bild der Armut in der BRD - ein Überblick, in: Beilage zur Zeitschrift DAS PARLAMENT 31-32/1995; G. E. Zimmermann, Neue Armut und neuer Reichtum. Zunehmende Polarisierung der materiellen Lebensbedingungen im vereinten Deutschland, in: Gegenwartskunde, 44. Jg., Heft 1, S. 5-18.

10 EDUCATION AND TRAINING

Education is part of the federal system in Germany. The 13 Länder (states) and three *Stadtstaaten* (city states: Berlin, Bremen and Hamburg) have guaranteed autonomy on all matters of culture and education. The federal government provides only a general policy framework. The universities have a law setting out their basic framework (*Hochschulrahmengesetz*) which guarantees conformity among types of institution and leaving certificates.

In 1956, West Germans were spurred into action by the USSR's successful launch of Sputnik and by unfavourable comparisons with the education systems of other industrial countries. Comprehensive reform of schools and universities was initiated. Until the early 1960s, around 75 percent of all school leavers completed eight years of a first and second level primary school after which – at the age of 14 – they started their apprenticeships. Today, around 60 percent gain a certificate entitling them to go to university, or a leaving certificate from an intermediate school (*Realschule*). This expansion means that apprenticeships now begin at the age of eighteen. Girls benefitted more than boys.

In 1990, the unification of Germany created real problems. Both the institutions and the content of East German education were very different from those in the western Länder. East Germany had abolished the three step education system on the grounds that it was class based. In 1959, the ten year general polytechnic high school (*Polytechnische Oberschule*) had been introduced, as well as an extended high school (*Erweiterte Oberschule*) in which classes 11 and 12 worked towards the *Abitur* (the certificate required for entering university). The *Abitur* was gained a year earlier than in West Germany and by far fewer students.

The vocational school system is complex. All students must attend vocational school on a part time basis until they are 18 years old, unless they are attending another full time school. Vocational schools are at the centre of the traditional dual system: they provide theoretical training while the workplace provides practical training. There are now only about

350 recognized skilled jobs with apprenticeships attached, compared with a thousand in 1950. A few jobs predominate: car mechanics, electrical engineers, bricklayers, carpenters and industrial mechanics make up 25 percent of all male apprentices; practice nurses, clerical workers, shop assistants, dental nurses and hairdressers make up 35 percent of all female apprentices. The dual system is now moving towards a crisis. Fewer and fewer businesses are prepared to take on apprentices from a fear of the additional costs; and new technologies and globalization mean that the whole system of work and earnings is being restructured. Job security and long term career paths are both threatened.

Since the 1960s, the entire tertiary education sector has been expanded and restructured. Beginning with Bochum in 1963 the number of universities in Germany has doubled. Newly founded institutions like Konstanz or Bayreuth, Bamberg or Bochum, Trier or Düsseldorf have gained a high profile in a very short time, and because of their new methods of organization are very popular with students. Theological colleges, art and music academies and technical colleges have also multiplied, many being set up in smaller towns and more remote parts of the country.

Sources: Arbeitsgruppe Bildungsbericht am Max-Planck-Institut für Bildungsforschung, Das Bildungswesen in der Bundesrepublik Deutschland: Strukturen und Entwicklungen im Überblick, Hamburg 1994; Bundesministerium für Bildung, Wissenschaft, Forschung und Technologie, Hg., Grund- und Strukturdaten 1995/96, Bonn 1996; Globus in: DIE ZEIT v. 17.1.1997; Bundestagsdrucksachen 13/4261 u. 13/4498.

11 BELIEFS

There are two major Christian churches in Germany, the protestant church (*Evangelische Kirche in Deutschland* or EKD) and the Catholic Church (*Katholische Kirche*). In the mid 1990s each had about 28 million members, together accounting for about 70 percent of the population.

For historical reasons, the EKD is organized into 24 area churches, which come together to form the EKD's council and synod. The Catholic Church is divided into 6 archdioceses, 18 bishoprics and 4 episcopal authorities. There are a number of other Christian or old testament communities in Germany: members of the Greek and Russian Orthodox Churches, Seventh Day Adventists, Mormons, the New Apostolic Church and Jehovah's Witnesses. After the Christians, Muslims form the second largest religious group in Germany, of which 80 percent are Turkish. For historical reasons there are now very few Jews. There had been a substantial Jewish community before millions of Jews were executed during the period of National Socialism, 1930-45.

Since the Second World War, the separation between Catholics and Protestants has lost its significance. Large numbers of refugees and others expelled from their homes have not only ensured that Germany is a country of mixed religious beliefs, they have also encouraged more tolerance in private and public life. In 1939, Catholics accounted for a third of the population of the German Reich, Protestants about 60 percent. By 1950, Catholics made up 44 percent of the West German population, Protestants 52 percent. Protestant Prussia and its empire no longer existed, and from 1945 onwards religious beliefs were removed from party politics. The Nazi regime's fight against both the major churches brought them closer together after the war.

Nevertheless the split between Catholic and Protestant is still overt and tangible. There are many hospitals, high schools, colleges, academies and universities which are tied to one or other of these two major faiths. More important are the two huge church welfare organizations: the *Diakonisches Werk* (founded as the *Innere Mission* in 1848 and renamed in 1957) and the *Deutscher Caritasverband* (founded in 1897). After the state, these are the two largest employers in Germany.

There is no official state church in Germany but the links between church and state are still strong. This can be partly explained by the status of the two main churches in public law. Each church is entitled to charge a church tax from its members which is deducted from wages and salaries. In 1990, the founding Länder of German Protestantism, especially Thuringia (Thüringen) and Saxony-Anhalt (Sachsen-Anhalt), where Martin Luther had preached, became part of a unified Germany. Religious belief had changed totally in East Germany during 40 years of state promoted atheism. In 1945, over 90 percent of the population belonged to one of the two churches (10 percent were Catholic, 80 percent Protestant). By 1990, church membership had dropped to 30 percent (6 percent being Catholic, 25 percent Protestant).

During the last 25 years, sects and their like have joined the picture, especially individual youth sects and the Church of Scientology.

Sources:. Gabriel: Art. „Kirchen/Religionsgemeinschaften", in: B. Schäfers u. W. Zapf, Hg., Handwörterbuch zur Gesellschaft Deutschlands, Opladen 1997; M. Hartmann: Art. „Kirchen", in: W. Weidenfeld u. K. R. Korte, Hg., Handbuch zur deutschen Einheit, Bonn 1993; NRW-Lexikon. Politik. Gesellschaft. Wirtschaft. Recht. Kultur, Opladen 1996; Jugendwerk der deutschen Shell, Hg., Jugend '92, Bd. 2, Opladen 1992.

12 HEALTH

The health system is a mirror image of Germany's standard of living. First, it includes doctors (classified by 24 different specialties), hospitals, the social service centres of the welfare organizations and the various health administrations. Second, it includes the spas (with their sanatoriums and treatments), rehabilitation centres, and the preventative health measures undertaken within schools and businesses. Finally, there is the more indirect part of the health system: the university medical faculties, research institutions within and outside the universities, and the pharmaceutical industry with its own research laboratories.

This complex sector is responsible for the right to health of the whole population. It operates at both federal and Land level, deals with public and private health funds and insurances, and includes ministries for health administration and policy. In the wider sense, it is charged with the prevention of disease and accidents. If one were to judge success by the number of injuries sustained at work, the number of injuries and deaths in traffic accidents, and the alarming numbers of drug addicts, then it would have to be said that this has been limited. If social wellbeing is also part of its brief, its success can only be judged by the suicide rate. Although not all suicides can be explained by social factors, the differences between east and west are telling because national patterns (such as traditionally high suicide rates in Hungary) are removed from the equation. In 1992, the suicide rate in west Germany was 17 per 1000, while in the east it was 21 per 1000. The proportion of deaths following alcohol abuse are also very different: 5 per 1000 in west Germany compared with 11 per 1000 in the east.

The health system has achieved some successes: infant mortality has declined; since 1950, life expectancy has risen significantly; and diseases such as scarlet fever, diphtheria, polio, tuberculosis and venereal diseases have declined dramatically. It has also been successful in its fight against disease, since few illnesses lead directly to death. Heart and coronary disease account for half of all deaths in Germany, and cancers for a quarter.

The importance that Germans attach to health can be seen in the high levels of expenditure. This is backed up by the last microcensus on the health system in 1992, in which 7.5 million people declared themselves ill and 900,000 said they suffered from injuries sustained in accidents. At that time then, almost 12 percent of Germans considered that their health was inadequate. This was true of more women than men. On average women live six years longer than men, and are prone to more illnesses because of their greater age.

Since the health reforms of 1989 and 1993 and subsequent years, patients have been expected to contribute a higher share of the health system's escalating costs.

Sources: Globus Nr. 4052/1997; J. Mackay: Der Weltgesundheitsatlas, Bonn 1993; Stat. Bundesamt der Europäischen Gemeinschaft, Hg., Sozialporträt Europas, Luxemburg 1995.

13 CRIME

Much crime goes unreported, although how much varies greatly and depends on the nature of the crime. The amount of crime there is today leaves most people with a more or less permanent sense of anxiety. However, the incidence of crime is very uneven. Some places and times of day have relatively high crime rates: for example, underground trains, parks, and car parks, at night. Safety in public places and on public transport has deteriorated, largely because of the lack of social controls. However, the protection of children, women and elderly people is not sufficiently allowed for in town planning and building schemes.

Crime is a complex social phenomenon and a whole range of institutions is involved in its prevention and punishment. The police and the judiciary constitute a large part of what we call the state apparatus for dealing with crime. There are also numerous public and private security services though there are no precise numbers. There is some private provision, for example, against theft from people's homes, or of their cars or bicycles. There is also some private provision against physical attack, in the form of a wide range of insurance schemes which cover criminal offences. Finally, society has to reckon with various forms of anti-social behaviour that go on regularly within the bureaucracy, such as white collar crime.

Despite the many theories put forward about crime, responsibility for crime can usually be put down to two root causes: the personality problems of individuals or the problems of society itself. The first assumes that crime and deviant behaviour are caused by predisposition, poor socialization and other personality traits. The second holds social factors responsible: whole areas of cities may turn into slums (such as the 'no go' areas of some US cities), and may be driven into severe poverty; there may also be a complete failure of educational institutions and social controls. Some social-psychological theories take a midway position, looking at forms of prejudice and discrimination against minorities and arguing that they lead to oppression and violence.

In Germany, crime rates among foreigners, who represent 8.6 percent of the total population, remain controversial. But while the proportion of foreigners in German prisons is relatively high, it is also true that some groups of foreigners are liable to attract more attention from the various authorities. Some foreigners, of course, are more integrated into German society than others. Crime rates among long term residents or foreigners born in Germany are no higher than those of the German population.

Crime statistics reveal a further interesting point, that some people, depending on their age and gender, are more likely than others to be a victim of crime.

We have not been able to cover one further serious threat to society: organized crime involving drugs, the arms trade, or the trade in women.

Sources: Bundeskriminalamt Wiesbaden, Hg., Polizeiliche Kriminalstatistik Bundesrepublik Deutschland, Berichtsjahr 1994, Wiesbaden 1995; M. Fuchs, Waffenbesitz bei Kindern und Jugendlichen, in: H. Alemann, Hg., Mensch Gesellschaft! Lebenschancen und Lebensrisiken in der neuen Bundesrepublik, Opladen 1995; R. Geißler, Die Sozialstruktur Deutschlands, Opladen 1996; ders.: Das gefährliche Gerücht von der hohen Ausländerkriminalität, in: Beilage zur Wochenzeitung DAS PARLAMENT 35/1995, S. 30-39; H.-D. Schwind, Kriminologie. Eine praxisorientierte Einführung mit Beispielen, 8. Aufl., Heidelberg 1995; Süddeutsche Zeitung v. 11.3.1997; Demokratie ist verletzlich — Rechtsextremismus in Deutschland; Begleitheft zur Ausstellung des Bundesamtes für Verfassungsschutz, Köln.

14 COMMUNICATIONS

By media, we usually mean the print media (newspapers, magazines and books); acoustic media (broadly speaking, radio, records, cassettes, CDs); and audiovisual media (television and video, cable, videotext, teletext, Ceefax and so on). The last three of these are also known as 'new' media; being dependent on a computer screen (PC) and new forms of digital data capture, processing and networking.

Radio and television in Germany are still shaped by the concepts of the postwar Allied Powers on the matter of a free press within a democratic order. When West and East Germany were founded in 1949, many of the above media did not exist. In 1950, around 45 percent of all households had a radio. From then on, the media of the two Germanies became very different.

East Germany soon lost its free press. Out of the 39 daily newspapers that appeared regularly, two thirds were owned by the United German Socialist Party (SED or *Sozialistische Deutsche Einheitspartei*). The first West German television channel began broadcasting in 1952, the first East German channel in 1953. Television by no means ousted radio from a media scene which was becoming more mixed. From the 1950s onwards, the development of the transistor made radio more mobile as well as suitable for cars (virtually all cars now have radios). During the 1970s, radio became an even more popular means of communication, as third and fourth radio channels as well as city and regional radio stations were set up.

The growth of audiovisual and 'new ' media has had such a profound impact on individual consciousness, work, leisure, and society as a whole that we now say we live in an 'information and communication society'.

In 1986 there was, for West Germany, an almost revolutionary judgement on the media by the Federal Constitutional Court (*Bundes-verfassungsgericht*). This permitted private radio and television stations to broadcast alongside existing public channels. Since then the number of private channels has continued to rise.

Television has not led to the demise of radio, nor has it taken the place of the print media. Just the opposite: they are expanding as though they mutually enhance one another. This can be seen by a glance at a typical German newspaper kiosk: there is no cultural or other interest, no hobby, no area of information or entertainment that is not marketable through magazines. Bearing in mind that each copy of a tabloid newspaper is read on average by three people, daily newspapers are read by roughly 81 percent of those over 14 years old, or as many as 14 million people.

Ownership of the media is becoming more and more concentrated. This is true of all media, not just the press. In 1998, two public radio stations, SWF (*Südwestfunk*) and SDR (*Süddeutscher Rundfunk*) will be combined as SWR (*Südwestrundfunk*) with its headquarters in Stuttgart. When it comes to private radio stations, this concentration of ownership is even more significant. Worldwide information empires are emerging which are increasingly able to escape public control.

Sources: H. J. Kleinsteuber u. T. Rossmann, Hg., Europa als Kommunikationsraum, Opladen 1996; M. Pape u. D. Samland, Hg., Medienhandbuch - die Privaten: privater Hörfunk, privates Fernsehen, Neuwied u. a. 1996; H. Schatz, Art. „Massenmedien", in: Handwörterbuch des politischen Systems der Bundesrepublik Deutschland, 2. Aufl., Opladen 1993; H. F. Spinner, Informations- und Kommunikationsgesellschaft, in: B. Schäfers, Hg., Grundbegriffe der Soziologie, 4. Aufl., Opladen 1995; W. Weidenfield u. K.-R. Korte, Hg., Handbuch zur deutschen Einheit, Bonn 1994; Bundestagsdrucksache 12/8587; Jäschke Optimum Media, Prognos AG/MGM Publication Facts & Fiction 1/95; AG der Landesmedienanstalten, Hg., Jahrbuch der Landesmedienanstalten 1995/1996. Privater Hörfunk in Deuschland, München 1996.

15 FREE TIME

The idea of leisure as it is understood today came about with the growth of an industrial urban society. As work time became increasingly defined and controlled (the major objective of workers' movements from the middle of the nineteenth century) the amount of personal time available increased. After the First World War, the eight hour day was introduced, though still part of a six day week. From the 1950s onwards, the five day week became more and more common and a leisure industry began to develop. The standard of living could now be measured in material goods – by the quality of housing, and whether people owned a car, television set, refrigerator or washing machine. Going a step further, it could also be measured by the amount of free time people enjoyed. Between 1956 and 1980 the average working week for workers was reduced from 47.1 to 40 hours, and for white collar workers from 47.5 to 40 hours. The number of cars in West Germany rose from 4.5 million in 1960 to 30 million in 1988. The car was a prerequisite for many leisure activities, especially at weekends.

From the mid 1960s, sports like tennis, previously regarded as exclusive, were taken up much more widely. Germans began to take more frequent holidays and travel to ever more distant places. In 1972, 72 percent of households had a television set. Soon it would be available in virtually every home and became a major influence on the leisure habits of families with children. At the same time, hobbies and home maintenance became more popular, and more people acquired second homes. City tourism and festivals of all kinds (rock music, opera and so on) developed, as did the culture industry. Each year an increasing part of disposable income is spent on leisure goods and leisure activities.

An increase in the amount of time not spent working for wages does not always mean an increase in leisure time. Working women, for example, have very little leisure time since housework and looking after the family are not usually shared equally with men. The sick and those needing continuous care are usually looked after by relatives. Many young people have to earn their way through university as well as study. Chancellor Helmut Kohl once called Germany a 'collective leisure park', but for many people this is an irrelevant concept. Not just for women and students, but also for the growing numbers of long term unemployed, and foreigners deprived of many leisure activities because they cannot afford them. Nevertheless there are enough people with more than six weeks' annual holiday, and often two incomes per household, to make Germans the world champions of travel.

Interpretations of leisure vary greatly (how does one classify working in the garden for example?) as does leisure spending. However as far as holiday travel is concerned the gap between east and west Germany has rapidly closed. In 1992, 53.5 percent of west Germans and 51.5 percent of east Germans enjoyed a holiday of at least five days. Cars are used for 61 percent of all holiday trips.

Many people take on a great deal of unpaid work in their leisure time: in social welfare organizations, politics, or as school governors. In 1994, 18 percent of all adult Germans were involved in some voluntary work.

Sources: Basisdaten. Zahlen zur sozio-ökonomischen Entwicklung der Bundesrepublik Deutschland, bearb. v. R. Ermrich, Bonn-Bad Godesberg 1974; Bundestagsdrucksache 13/2652, Bonn 1996; G. Schulze, Die Erlebnisgesellschaft, 4. Aufl., Frankfurt a. M., New York 1993; Süddeutsche Zeitung v. 10.3.1997.

16 CLUBS AND ASSOCIATIONS

The right to form free clubs (*Vereine*) and associations (*Verbände*) is a vital link between all middle class and workers' movements for political emancipation. In Germany, this right is enshrined in Article 9 of the Basic Law.

Clubs play a major role in German life – especially in small communities. They turn a complex society into a close social network. They also provide a vital means of social integration, for foreigners as well as Germans, and they are especially important for young people.

Their origins and traditions are middle class, so it is not surprising that there are as yet considerably fewer clubs in the eastern Länder than there are in the west. In East Germany, social and cultural life and leisure activities were organized on a completely different basis, with the workplace at the centre. Membership of all types of club is therefore markedly lower than it is in the west.

Clubs and associations are usually considered together since they both mainly rely on voluntary membership. However, associations tend to focus mainly on political and professional interests, whereas clubs tend to focus on leisure. A clear division between the two is impossible. They are not only organized in the same way, but some clubs are also active in the political and professional world.

The Civil Code (BGB or *Bürgerliche Gesetzbuch*) distinguishes between clubs with business interests and those without. To set up a club and run it as a legal entity, it is necessary to get on to the register of *Vereine* at the district court. Most clubs, including sports clubs, are registered, as well as 'citizens' initiatives' formed for a particular purpose (see note to **33. Political Participation**). Sports clubs, music clubs, shooting clubs, and also clubs concerned with local traditions such as carnivals, are hugely important to individual members because they provide a way of participating in the social and cultural life of the community. In sports clubs, for instance, it is still customary to remain a member even after age rules out active involvement.

The sports clubs are the largest *Vereine*, and these are brought together within an umbrella organization, the Deutscher Sportbund. In 1995, it had over 22 million members within 85,519 sports clubs. This means that every fourth German is a member of a sports club. Almost five million members are under 15 years old, with large differences between east and west Germany. Sports club membership is still mainly a male affair and men constitute 61 percent of all members. The Deutscher Fußballbund has the largest number of members in the Deutscher Sportbund. In 1995 it had 5.7 million members, a quarter of all paying members. Only 11 percent of football club members are female.

The Deutscher Sängerbund is the umbrella organization for the many singing clubs or choirs which are so popular across Germany. In 1995, it had almost two million members within 17,520 choirs. Altogether there are about 21,000 choirs which belong to regional singing associations: 44 percent are men's choirs, 34 percent are mixed choirs, 10 percent are women's choirs, and 12 percent are young people's choirs and boys' choirs.

Associations also have a voluntary membership. The best known are the political parties, the trade unions, the central organizations of employers, the professional associations (such as the Farmers' Association or *Deutscher Bauernverband*), and the central social welfare organizations. Finally associations also include special interest groups such as the ADAC (German Automobile Association) which in March 1997 was one of Germany's largest *Verbände*, with 13.5 million members.

Sources: H. Best, Hg., Vereine in Deutschland. Vom Geheimbund zur freien gesellschaftlichen Organisation, Bonn 1993; Informationen über Ebersteinburg: Umfrage d. Verf., Herbst 1996; Taschenbuch des öff. Lebens Deutschlands, 1996/97, S. 715ff.

17 TRAFFIC

The growth of all forms of traffic has meant that towns and cities have become more densely populated, urban areas have expanded, and increased distances between home and work have become possible.

The railway system is much smaller than it was at its peak. In 1992, there were 41,000 km of railway line, whereas before the First World War there were 63,000 km.

Since the 1930s, roads have been the dominant form of transport. Starting in 1950, West Germany quickly built a modern road network, basing it on the prewar *Reichsautobahn*. By 1990, the national road network in West Germany covered 174,000 km; the autobahns, 9000 km; and municipal and city roads 325,000 km. In 1990, in East Germany there were 1900 km of autobahns, and 77,000 km of municipal and city roads. The number of cars has likewise increased. In 1949 in West Germany, there were 500,000 cars; by 1988, the number had risen above 30 million. In East Germany there were about 4 million cars at the end of 1989; by the end of 1992, this had risen to 6 million.

The density of the traffic and lax speed limits mean that the number of traffic deaths per year in Germany is extremely high. About a third of fatalities occur in urban areas, and a quarter of the victims are between 18 and 24 years old. A driving licence can be obtained at the age of 18.

For health and environmental reasons the bicycle has enjoyed a revival since the early 1970s. The recent growth of bicycle lanes shows that the boom is continuing. The bicycle, however, is not a primary means of transport. It is an add-on rather than a replacement for the car.

Little is being done to counter the problems created by private cars. When local public transport expands its main impact is that it adds to mobility. The growth of suburbs and the distances involved make it difficult for public transport to be profitable. As in major cities elsewhere, the safety of public transport is an additional problem, particularly in underground trains late at night. The emphasis on individuals and individual needs together with the increased complexity of work patterns mean that no major reduction in the number or use of cars can be foreseen.

Sources: W. Brög u. E. Erl, Socialdata München, Round Table 102, Nr. 7, München o. J.; Bundesverkehrsministerium, Hg., Verkehr in Zahlen 1995; Globus Nr. 3989/1997; Bundestagsdrucksache 13/4683.

18 EMPLOYMENT

'Normal' work, regulated by contract, with fixed working hours, sickness benefit, social security contributions and so on, is often referred to as the first labour market. It excludes a great deal of other work done, much of which is unpaid. It excludes housework and caring for the family, work that is necessary for the 'reproduction' of the workforce and mainly done by women. It excludes voluntary work. It excludes the millions whose income is below the limit at which social security contributions become payable, currently DM610. Finally it excludes all work done in the informal economy.

The numbers employed include the self employed and independent professionals such as lawyers and accountants. The unemployed are people not in work or people looking for work. 'Family helpers', such as farmers' wives, have no formal employment of their own. The term self employed refers to those who manage their own business or farm as proprietors or leaseholders, as well as everyone employed in a freelance capacity. In Germany, the proportion of paid workers in the total population is 48.8 percent.

Work and employment are the most important indicators of social change. Since 1950 there has been a big decline in the professions and in the number of family helpers – particularly in agriculture, but also in the rest of the primary sector: forestry and fishing. Until 1970, the number of workers in the secondary sector (manufacturing, energy, mining and construction) continued to rise, but since then most gains have been in the tertiary sector (services, trade, transport, state and municipal institutions). The growth of the 'information society' has led to so many new jobs in the media that these may be reclassified as a fourth sector of the economy.

In employment by sector, there is surprisingly little difference between west and east Germany and the numbers are moving still closer together. In the west, the number of women workers has been rising since 1980, whereas in the east, the number has just as dramatically dropped. In East Germany, women were encouraged to work and in 1990, 50.5 percent of all workers were women. The number of self employed has increased in the new Länder, though the numbers are much smaller than in the old Länder.

Sources: R. Geißler, Die Sozialstruktur Deutschlands, 2. Aufl., Opladen 1996; St. Mau, Objektive Lebensbedingungen und subjektives Wohlbefinden, in: W. Zapf u. R. Habich, Hg., Wohlfahrtsentwicklung im vereinten Deutschland, Berlin 1996, S. 51-78; Statistisches Bundesamt, Hg., Reihe 4.1.1, Fachserie 1: Bevölkerung und Erwerbstätigkeit, Wiesbaden 1996.

19 WAGES

German employees are paid wages according to formal agreements and wage rates are nearly always negotiated. Almost 90 percent of all paid workers are directly dependent on their employers. White collar workers are paid salaries, but there are even finer distinctions in terminology. Civil servants receive 'income'; the self employed receive income defined as gain; lawyers and doctors are paid honorariums; artists receive fees, or *Gage*.

Whatever the name, the most important distinction to be made is between gross and net income. Taxation levels determine the difference between the two. Employees who are unmarried and childless fall into tax class 1 and relatively speaking pay the highest rate of tax.

Wages and salaries may be part of a national or regional agreement or may be independently negotiated. Monthly wages are the only source of income for the majority of workers. Every time there is a proposed increase in sickness or pension contributions there are tough negotiations between the various parties. In the last few years, employers have become more and more concerned about the cost of staff in addition to wages. Such costs include statutory employers' costs: such as social security contributions, paid bank holidays and sickness pay; plus those additional costs that are agreed by the company: such as paid leave of various kinds, holiday pay, extra payments (a 13th or even 14th month salary for example), company pensions, and profit sharing schemes. Germany spends more on these additional staff costs, and German workers have longer holidays, than anywhere else in the world. In a company with 10 or more employees, these additional costs are equivalent to 80 percent of wages and salaries in the old Länder and 70 percent in the new.

Women tend to work in low paid jobs such as hairdressing, beauty treatment, hotels and bars, cleaning services, or as sales assistants. More men, on the other hand, work in the highly paid jobs such as insurance, financial services, the media, architecture, and as technicians and programmers. As yet there are very few women in top jobs or in management. Despite measures to bridge this gap and although some women are now being promoted, there has still been little change over the last 30 years. In the political parties and parliaments, only specially designed quota systems have improved the proportion of women managers.

The gap in gross salaries of east and west will doubtless continue for some years, in the public sector as well as the private sector. The eastern Länder have less economic power and their productivity is lower, but the east German economy cannot afford to lose its competitive edge. In the meantime, the cost of mail, freight and so on have increased and the cost of living, especially rent, is going up. There is much criticism of the income gap between east and west.

Sources: A. Hadler. M. E. Domsch, Frauen auf dem Weg in Spitzenpositionen der Wirtschaft? Eine Bestandsaufnahme für die Bundesrepublik Deutschland, in: Beilage zur Wochenzeitung DAS PARLAMENT, B 6, 1994; R. Hauser, Die Entwicklung der Einkommensverteilung in den neuen Bundesländern seit der Wende, in: M. Diewald, K.-U. Mayer, Hg., Zwischenbilanz der Wiedervereinigung, Opladen 1996, S. 165-188; V. Steiner, F. Kraus, Aufsteiger und Absteiger in der ostdeutschen Einkommensverteilung, in: M. Diewald, K.-U. Mayer, a.a.O., S. 189-214.

20 UNEMPLOYMENT

In a society heavily oriented towards work and performance, losing one's job, or being unable to find a job after leaving school, university, or vocational training can cause severe stress. A job is the most important source of livelihood and the means of providing for sickness and old age. The lack of a job can strain social relationships until they reach breaking point.

Over 50 percent of the unemployed have been dismissed. Twenty percent have given notice, the next most common reason. One of the main causes of youth unemployment is the lack of jobs available after training.

Levels of unemployment vary greatly between men and women, between the different age groups, between the various regions and the Länder, and depending on the time of year. The high unemployment level in Bremen, shown in the map, is largely due to changes in the region's shipping and fishing industries. Civil servants are not threatened by unemployment. Public sector workers may be protected from dismissal after working for an agreed number of years. Manual and private sector workers, school leavers, university graduates, trainees, women and older workers are most at risk of being unemployed, and find it most difficult to get jobs.

Over the last few years, having to cope with unemployment has become an almost normal experience. Long term unemployment and redundancy through early retirement have become even bigger problems. The unification of Germany introduced unheard of levels of unemployment which, for workers in the east in particular were a completely new experience. In former East Germany the right to a job had been written into the constitution. This is one of the reasons why productivity in East Germany was less than 40 percent that of West Germany.

Official unemployment statistics understate the extent of the problem. The unemployment figures would be much higher if they included people retraining, or those with temporary jobs which are part of job creation schemes. They would be higher still if they included all those not registered as unemployed or who have not made it known officially that they are looking for work.

The fight against unemployment and the need for social security are major social questions. For workers' parties and trade unions they have been the prime focus since the middle of the last century. The problems are not confined to Germany but are common to Europe as a whole. The right to protection against dismissal has been eroded and job risks fall more and more on individuals.

The rise in unemployment has recently been accompanied by overall economic growth. Some studies argue that if unemployment is to come down, annual economic growth must exceed 2.5 percent.

Sources: H. Friedrich, M. Wiedemeyer, Arbeitslosigkeit — ein Dauerproblem im vereinten Deutschland?, 2. Aufl., Opladen 1994; Globus Nr. 3964/1997; Landesarbeitsamt Niedersachsen-Bremen, Hg., Informationen zum Arbeitsmarkt des Landes Bremen, Pressemitteilung v. 7.11.1996; Datenreport 1994, S.92.

21 INDUSTRIAL RELATIONS

Cooperation between capital and labour, employers and employees, and employers' associations and trade unions, is at the heart of industrial relations. As in any other free democracy, such cooperation is based on the right to negotiate the terms and conditions of work.

The principles of industrial relations in Germany are laid down in Article 9 of the Basic Law, though their precise form changes along with society. There are many controversial changes now taking place: the result of privatization (of railways and the mail for example), the globalization of capital and assets, and the impact of European Union law.

Labour relations are also influenced by single company agreements between works councils and management. Works councils now also have considerable legal power in any negotiation with a trade union: they allow employers to escape from fixed regional agreements, and enable on site agreements based on local conditions. Trade unions rightly object that works councils are the beginning of the end for the workers' movement and workers' representation. They also argue that it was the unity of the trade union movement, founded after the Second World War, that played such a vital part in establishing the social welfare state, in creating social progress, and in bringing about a significant reduction in the number of strikes.

Workers are allowed to use strikes as a weapon, but only after all sides have agreed a complex procedure. In 1980, a supreme court judgement confirmed the right of employers to respond to a strike with a lockout.

For the unions, the right to take part in negotiations is a core demand. Miners won full negotiating rights in 1951, but other industries did not achieve this until 1976. Other laws on the right to take part in negotiations (in the public sector, for example) were introduced in the 1950s and have since been revised several times.

Some hope – and some fear – that new ways of organizing companies and businesses, new forms of communication (as a result of new technology), and new and ever more complex patterns of European and global capital, will have a profound effect on the classic forms of labour relations, conflict resolution and participation.

High unemployment and other economic changes have led to a major drop in trade union membership. In the eastern Länder, many workers joined trade unions after unification but large numbers are now leaving again. This is not just the result of very high unemployment. It also reflects the fact that in the east, only 50 percent of workers are covered by regional pay agreements.

Sources: H.-H. Hartwich, Der Flächentarifvertrag. Instrument und Symbol kollektivrechtlicher Arbeitsbeziehungen in Deutschland, in: Gegenwartskunde, 46. Jg./1997, H. 1, S. 101-134; Globus Nr. 3707/1996; Bundesvorstand DGB, Auskunft April 1997.

22 SOCIAL SECURITY

Germany is committed to being a social welfare state, and is therefore committed to an active social policy. Bismarck first began to establish social legislation in 1883, which means that Germany can claim to have one of the oldest social welfare states in the world. The German constitution guarantees the equality of all its citizens, but this should include social equality. The social welfare state should mean more than personal security, job security, and an old age pension. It should also safeguard the integration of all citizens into society. Levels of social inequality should be no higher than is appropriate to the common good and social justice.

Demands for the Americanization of work are testing the limits of the Basic Law. Social inequality, given different educational levels, earnings and general success, should be permitted only if they do not exclude any citizens from the mainstream of culture, society and the economy. Germans strongly believe that social security and social peace are invaluable 'social capital'.

Spending on social welfare includes:

• General payments (two thirds of the entire budget): these include the pensions fund, state sickness and accident fund, child benefit, and education benefit.

• Payments by employers (9 percent): including sickness pay for up to six weeks and company pensions.

• Social service benefits (9 percent): including income support, youth support, educational grants and housing benefit.

• Other: special payments, such as pensions for farmers; civil service provisions (especially pensions); compensation payments (needed, for example, to equalize the welfare burdens of the Länder); and indirect benefits (such as tax benefits and public housing support).

The level of contributions is the ratio of all social security contributions to gross domestic product (GDP). For some years, this ratio has been one to three. How the social security budget is financed is one of the most controversial questions of the moment. About two thirds is financed by employers and employees and the state redistributes these funds. In the last few years the state has also redistributed considerable funds acquired for other purposes (for example, pensions income). But these reserves have been swallowed up by unexpected burdens: high unemployment, unification, and the cost of supporting newly arrived ethnic Germans, asylum seekers, and war refugees.

After unification in 1990, East Germany's social welfare system had to be integrated with that of the west. This has improved the position of pensioners in the eastern Länder.

The reorganization of the social welfare state and the safeguarding of its main principles have become urgent and this process must take the laws of the European Union into account. There are fundamental problems to resolve: the links between social security and work; the protection of basic social wellbeing through other means than income support; and the provision of finance covering federal legislation, given that municipal budgets are already overstrained.

Sources: Globus in: Süddeutsche Zeitung v. 5.2.1997; Der Spiegel Nr. 20/1996; Bevölkerung und Erwerbstätigkeit, Fachserie 1, Reihe 4.1.1. Stand und Entwicklung der Erwerbstätigkeit 1995, hrsg. v. Statistischen Bundesamt, S. 106.

23 SAFETY NETS

Income support, according to German law, must be granted to anyone without the financial means of survival. This legislation is described as the 'net beneath the net'.

There are two forms of income support, both of which may be either temporary or ongoing. The first is general income support or welfare benefit: this includes regular payments for food, accommodation and personal hygiene, and less frequent payments for clothing and household goods. The second is income support for specific emergencies or special situations (such as emergency personal allowances, disability allowances, or sickness benefit). Three quarters of those on income support receive welfare benefit. However 63 percent of total expenditure on welfare goes towards special support, of which disability allowances account for a very high proportion.

There are set limits to income support which are also used as a measure of income related poverty. These are based on day to day needs, housing, special circumstances and insurance contributions. At the end of 1996, the limit for Germany as a whole was DM523. Yet the limit for a single person in Baden-Württemberg was almost double this, or DM1114.

In 1993, 5 million people received income support, about 6 percent of the total population. Many of those who are entitled to income support do not claim it.

The cost of income support has been escalating. There has been a rise in long term unemployment, in the number of single parents, and in the number of young couples with children unable to fend for themselves. In 1993, 1.53 million people under 15 years old received income support, amounting to 27 percent of all recipients. Such high figures were not anticipated. In contrast, the poverty of old people has been greatly reduced – in the east as well as the west – largely because of major increases in pensions.

Child benefits are a very big part of the social welfare budget. They include all legal benefits available for children or young people. They include for example all benefits laid out in the Federal Youth Plan (*Bundesjugendplan*). This plan provides educational assistance for children not living with their parents: children who are in residential homes or in fulltime care with other families.

Sources: R. Hauser u. a., Ungleichheit und Sozialpolitik, Opladen 1996; G. E. Zimmermann, Art. „Armut", in: Handwörterbuch der Gesellschaft Deutschlands, hg. v. B. Schäfers u. W. Zapf, Opladen 1997.

24 ECONOMIC FOUNDATIONS

Gross domestic product (GDP), which measures the production of goods and services over a given period, is one of the best guides to the state of the economy and standards of living. There are three methods of calculating a country's GDP: by calculating the value of all goods and services produced by each sector of the economy, this being the gross value added; or by calculating the value of goods and services consumed; or, finally, by comparing the total value added to the economy with total income from paid work.

Price changes are factored in according to inflation rates, allowing comparison over time. In 1994, west Germany's GDP was 2.7 times what it was in 1960. Or, put another way, in 1994 west Germany produced 2.7 times more goods and services than it did in 1960. This was due to increased productivity, changes within the various sectors of the economy, and an increase in the number of jobs.

Changes in the relative power of the economic sectors have been a major cause of social change. In West Germany in 1950, the primary sector (agriculture, forestry and fishing) produced 9.1 percent of GDP, whereas in 1966 this had slumped to 1.1 percent. During the same period, the tertiary sector (services, trade, transport and so on) grew from 46.6 percent to 65.4 percent.

There are big differences in GDP between the Länder and the regions, and especially between east and west. In the east, unemployment is much higher, wages and salaries are only three quarters that of their western counterparts, and a higher percentage of the workforce is employed in the primary sector.

The division between domestic spending and government spending has also changed considerably. There have been major efforts to reduce government spending for some years.

The total volume of production has an impact on income. Currently, three quarters of all income is created by employees – industrialization and urbanization have led to a major fall in the numbers of self employed. The remainder comes from the self employed and from savings and wealth (from capital, for example, and from interest on rents and leases).

The self employed are 9 percent of all workers but earn a quarter of all income. However the many self employed people, such as grocers or people who lease petrol stations, earn relatively little. There are very big differences between east and west Germany in the proportion of income generated by the self employed and by savings and wealth. This is scarcely surprising. Until 1990, East Germany was a planned socialist economy.

'Purchasing power parities' are an index which reflects differences in purchasing power. They are used to provide a more accurate method of comparing national incomes.

Sources: Globus Nr. 3990/1997; Stat. Jb. 1996, S. 637; Gablers Wirtschaftslex., 12. Ausgabe, Bd. I, Sp. 2789.

25 TRADE

Germany depends on its exports and therefore on its foreign trade. It is necessary to distinguish not only between foreign and internal trade, but also between retail and wholesale trade. There has been a huge increase in trade, not just because of an increase in goods, but also because they are being shipped further and further away.

The number of small corner shops has noticeably slumped. In 1979 there were only 346,000, more than a hundred thousand fewer than in 1960. At the same time, chain stores and shopping centres on greenfield sites have mushroomed, very often at the expense of the inner cities.

After the Second World War, Germany had to recreate its export markets afresh. In June 1948, a year before West Germany was founded, currency and economic reforms allowed goods and money to begin flowing. International agreements were set up to guarantee Germany's rapid entry into world trade. They formed the basis for the economic miracle of the 1950s and 1960s. In 1951, Germany joined the GATT, a general agreement on customs and trade that had been formed by 23 countries in 1947. In 1952, Germany became a member of the International Monetary Fund (IMF), set up by the Bretton Woods agreement of 1944, to provide stable exchange rates for international currencies. It was only in 1971 that this system was replaced by a system of freely convertible currencies.

West Germany's trade received a major boost when it became a member of the European Coal and Steel Community, founded 1951, and a further boost when it joined the European Economic Community, founded 1957. The majority of German exports go to European countries, and in particular to EU member states.

Until 1990, East Germany's trade developed along very different lines. The East German Mark had been non convertible, and West Germany had counted its trade with East Germany as foreign trade. Most of East German foreign trade had been conducted primarily with CMEA/COMECON countries of the Eastern bloc, particularly the USSR. After unification in 1990, East Germany was included in West Germany's international trade agreements, and completely new institutions for managing both internal and foreign trade had to be created. East German retail and wholesale trade, largely defunct before 1990, has now been taken over by new trade organizations. Since CMEA/COMECON was dissolved, the markets have been gradually opening up to global trade.

It is necessary to distinguish between general trade and special trade. Special trade excludes foreign goods which are to be re-exported. Exports are therefore mainly calculated on the basis of special trade, since this avoids including goods not produced in Germany that would falsify the real balance of trade. Imports are meant to include all imported goods, so these are mainly calculated on the basis of general trade, or all foreign goods coming into Germany.

The first stage of economic and monetary union (EMU) takes place within the EU in 1999, and the new Euro coins should be in place by 2002. The Euro will have an impact on trade, not just because the cash machines will need to be reset, but because of new trade options within Europe and beyond.

Sources: Frankfurter Allgemeine Zeitung v. 31.1.1997; Globus in: Süddeutsche Zeitung v. 19.2. 1997; Datenreport 1995, S. 308. Globus Nr. 3998/1997; Stat. Jb. 1995, S. 282.

26 INVESTMENT AND ECONOMIC POWER

Capitalism, thanks to colonialism, industrialization and, in particular, globalization, has left economic power concentrated in few hands. In Germany, anti-monopoly legislation dates back to the 1870s. It was a time when ideological debate was reaching a climax: how could society, the state and the economy protect the individual from exploitation and from other potentially damaging effects of economic power?

With industrialization, the growing economic power of business became clear from the diverse forms of its disposable 'capital': investment trusts, shares, bonds and so on. In Germany, the banks also acquired economic power, their relationships with business becoming an increasingly complex and interdependent web, fairly incomprehensible to the outsider.

Over recent decades there have been significant changes. Money, stock and capital markets have strengthened and concentrated their economic power. The main economic sectors have become more integrated and have also developed stronger international links. Since the 1980s, the growth of privatization (for example in Germany, the privatization of rail, telecommunications and post) has increased exposure to competition in the open market.

West Germany was founded as a 'social market economy'. Key industries were nationalized, as set out in the Ahlener Programme of the Christian Democratic Union (CDU) in February 1947. Though this was intended to prevent the concentration of economic power, the effect was quite the opposite. Currency and credit markets became increasingly dependent upon individual private investors and international interests, and the national debt continued to rise. National and international money and credit markets, currency and stock markets may have been removed from political influence but they are still sensitive to politicians and political events.

All this has led to increasing inequality in the distribution of disposable wealth: in banking and trade, capital centres, stock exchanges, the media, as well as new centres of economic power such as software for new technology. The decline in investment by foreign companies in Germany, coupled with a rise in investment by German companies abroad, is seen to be a problem.

Furthermore, it has become clear that Germans are not naturally drawn to owning or trading in shares. Of the big industrial nations, only Italy has a lower proportion of private shareholders than Germany. The highest proportion is in the USA.

Sources: Der Bürger im Staat, hg. von der Landeszentrale für politische Bildung Baden-Württemberg, Red. H.-G. Wehling, 47. Jg., Heft 1, 1997, „Die Macht der Banken"; Globus Nr. 3686/1996; DIE ZEIT v. 4.10.1996; P. Windorf u. J. Beyer: Kooperativer Kapitalismus, in: Kölner Zeitschrift für Soziologie und Sozialpsychologie, Jg. 47, Heft 1/1995.

27 AGRICULTURE

More than half of Germany's total land is given over to agriculture: 200,000 sq km out of 357,000 sq km. But since industrialization, the proportion of agricultural workers and agriculture's share of gross domestic product (GDP), have both been in continual decline. In 1949, when West Germany was founded, about 25 percent of all workers were agricultural workers. Now only 3 percent work in the whole of the primary sector: agriculture, forestry and fishing.

Agriculture's share of GDP has declined even more dramatically: from 9.1 per cent in West Germany in 1950 to about 1 percent today. Nevertheless Germany is self sufficient in basic foods (grain/bread, meat, dairy products) and is therefore an agricultural exporter. Agriculture's share of GDP is so low because agriculture is subsidized (in 1995, by 5 billion DM) and because agricultural produce is usually sold at below the cost of production.

Since the Second World War, in East as well as West Germany, agriculture has changed completely. The traditional farm has been replaced by highly specialized land use and large scale animal farming. Since 1950, rye and barley production per hectare has doubled and other grain production has trebled. Milk production per cow (now about 5000 litres per year) has also doubled.

The pressures of the global market, and since 1958 of the European Common Market, have led to agricultural practices hostile to the environment. Fertilizers are overused and mass animal farming has introduced new health risks. Since the mid 1970s, some organic farming has been developed with support from the environmental movement, but its share of total production is low. Growing protests against genetic engineering and mass animal farming may bring about radical change over the next few years.

East German agriculture was managed on a very different basis from farms in the West. East Germany's large, state-owned enterprises and cooperatives covered vast areas of land. After unification, these became registered cooperatives.

Germans harbour strong feelings for their forests, which provided the emotional roots of Germany's strong environmental movement. It is not widely known that there is now 30 percent more forest land in Germany than there was in medieval or early modern times. The major change has been in the quality of the forests. Popular mixed forest has been cut back and there has been widespread growth of fast growing conifers. Conifers now account for three quarters of annual timber production. As a result of the Federal Forest Law (*Bundeswaldgesetz*) the forestry sector now has a legal obligation to maintain forest protection and recreation in perpetuity. This has significantly reduced concern about dying forests.

The fishing industry has also seen immense change. The North Sea and the Baltic Sea provide the biggest share of the German fish catch. Surprisingly, the largest individual catch is mussels (about 25 percent of the total); and Germany's favourite fish, herrings, are only the second largest. One seventh of the total comes from freshwater fishing in Germany's large lakes.

Sources: Agrarbericht 1996, Agrar- und ernährungspolitischer Bericht der Bundesregierung, Bundestagsdrucksache 13/3680, Bonn 1996; Bundesministerium für Ernährung, Landwirtschaft und Forsten, Hg., Stat. Jb. über Ernährung, Landwirtschaft und Forsten, verschied. Jahre; M. Fritzler, Ratgeber für den bewußten Einkauf, Bonn 1997; Globus Nr. 3943/1997; Globus in: Süddeutsche Zeitung v. 12.12.1996.

28 ENERGY

Energy, like transport and communications, is vital to industrial development. As a collective term it refers to all sources of energy used for cooking, heating, transport, manufacturing or making jobs easier. Until the beginning of the industrial era, only natural sources of energy were available: water, wind, wood, and fossil fuels. Coal, oil and gas came into use in the nineteenth century. Nuclear power dates only from 1950.

Today's chief sources of energy in the industrial world, coal, oil and gas, are all non renewable. In Germany as in many other countries, oil is the dominant source of energy (although in East Germany this was lignite). Since the nineteenth century, competition for energy has become a major cause of conflict and war. The growth of the environmental movement, has meant that forms of energy and energy consumption have become matters for strong political debate, especially with regard to town planning and housing. Nuclear power has been controversial for a longer period.

The environmental movement has developed powerful campaigns in favour of alternative energy sources such as the sun, wind and water. But reviews of alternative energy are sobering. While in some situations they make sense, they are by no means an adequate substitute. Electric cars – Germany has conducted the largest experiment in the world – have not yet provided a solution. They may minimize pollution and noise, but are still a great deal more expensive than other types of car.

The hole in the ozone layer, like many long term energy problems, is so far unresolved. There is no safe site, anywhere in the world, for highly radioactive waste to be stored indefinitely. In Germany, sites for disposing of low or medium grade radioactive waste, such as saltmines, are politically contentious and questioned by scientists.

Energy policy in Germany faces many major difficulties. In contrast to France, it would be virtually impossible to expand nuclear energy. Heavy subsidies for the coal mining industry are highly unlikely to continue. In the long term oil poses problems because it is non renewable. Alternative forms of energy have not yet proved themselves. And hydropower as an additional source of energy has very limited potential. For Germany the future lies in increased energy savings, in improved technology and in more efficient distribution. Imports of electricity from Europe, and gas from even further afield, will continue to increase. In 1997, the federal government was developing new energy legislation which recognizes that energy is a global commodity.

Sources: Globus Nr. 3915/1997 und Nr. 3982/1997; H. Köppen, Brauchen wir eine Energiesteuer? in: Gegenwartskunde, 45. Jg., Heft 4, 1996, S. 541-552; J. Seager, Der Öko-Atlas, 2. Aufl. Neuausgabe, Bonn 1997; Frankfurter Rundschau v. 10.2.1997.

29 WASTE

The disposal of waste has become a big social problem, not just for private households but for industry, hospitals, the military and public bodies. It has led to new terms such as recycling, and DSD (*Duales System Deutschland* or Dual System). New forms of disposal have also become necessary. It has become clear that large quantities of plastics and other non compostable waste (electrical goods, refrigerators, batteries, etc) should not simply be buried in landfill sites, burned or dumped in the deep sea. While such practices may still go on, there is now at least a widespread consciousness of potential, long term damage to the environment.

The vast majority of Germans live in cities or towns and are unable to compost their waste. But even rural, village or farming communities create large quantities of waste that are not biodegradable.

Recycling allows certain forms of waste to be reintegrated into the production process. In 1991, a recycling law was passed which set new limits on the quantity of packaging materials manufacturers are allowed to use. This law also resulted in the separation of household waste into compostable kitchen waste, plastics and other waste. Paper and glass were already being collected separately. The DSD was then founded, a private company which collects, sorts and reuses packaging. The term 'dual' refers to the fact that the DSD handles both collection and delivery. The green dot (*Grüne Punkt*) was introduced to identify packaging materials suitable for recycling. In order to use the green dot, companies have to pay the DSD a licence fee.

A new law on waste recycling and disposal was introduced in October 1995. Its purpose is to restructure waste production and consumption to the point where the need for waste disposal actually disappears. It is hoped that by inculcating a new sense of product responsibility, the costs of waste disposal can gradually be moved back into the original cost of production.

In 1995, around 65.5 kg of recycleable packaging per head was being collected. Within a very short time, recycling rates shot up: for paper, to around 90 percent, for glass, 82 percent. Even the recycling of plastics improved. It became possible to break the plastics down into liquids and gases and use them to recreate new ones.

Even with all these measures, the waste mountains cannot be reduced without harming the environment. After unification, East Germany's totally inadequate waste dumping system became an environmental headache for the newly unified Germany. According to an European Union (EU) guideline of 1994, the 15 members of the EU have to dispose of waste within their own borders. Though strong controls are supposed to be in place, some countries allow waste exports to travel as far as China. But even in Germany, a new black market in illegal waste exports has developed – yet another element of widespread 'environmental crime'.

Sources: Frankfurter Entsorgungsbetriebe und Umlandverband Frankfurt: Auskunft März 1997; Globus Nr. 3751/1996; Umweltbundesamt, Hg., Was sie schon immer über Abfall und Umwelt wissen wollten, Stuttgart 1993; Umweltgutachten 1996 der Bundesregierung, Bundestagsdrucksache 13/4108, Bonn 1996; (für einzelne Hinweise danke ich Dr. Rudolf Kasper, Baden-Baden).

30 FEDERAL GOVERNMENT

Article 20 of the Basic Law describes Germany as a 'democratic and social federal state' and Article 28 adds that it is a 'republican, democratic and social legal state'. Germany has been shaped by the principles of federalism. The Länder (founded in 1945-46) are part of the federal state, as are the urban and rural districts (*Kreise*) and the municipalities (*Gemeinden*). The Länder are separate states which have joined together in a federation. In so doing, they relinquish part of their rights as states, such as the right to control their currency, foreign policy, or defence.

Article 70 of the Basic Law gives the Länder the right to pass laws wherever the Basic Law does not give legislative power to the federal government. The Basic Law goes on to differentiate between an exclusive federal legislation and legislation which requires the consent of the Bundesrat, representing the Länder. The various federal authorities (listed in the table on page 91-92) are located right across the country, a fact which sums up very clearly the decentralized and federal nature of Germany.

There are two parliamentary bodies, the Bundestag and the Bundesrat. The Basic Law states that all power comes from the people and is executed by the people, through elections to the legislature, the executive and the judiciary. It is the classic form of separation of powers for mutual control. Before unification, there were 519 seats in the Bundestag. The current Bundestag, which ends in 1998, has 656 seats officially, but 672 members. This is explained by *Überhangmandate* (see note to **31. Elections**).

The Länder are represented through the Bundesrat, which has 68 seats. As in the European Parliament, the number of representatives cannot be entirely proportional to population if participation by the small Länder and city states is to be protected. There is a steep ratio between the population of the smallest Land (Bremen with a population of 680,000) and the largest (North Rhine Westphalia with a population of 17.8 million).

It is the municipalities *Gemeinden*) that influence day to day lives and are responsible for the physical, cultural and social wellbeing of citizens.

At the next level of government, the urban and rural district councils (*Kreise*) are independent local authorities. Rural councils are particularly important because they provide the hospitals, income support and so on, which are beyond the capacity of the smaller municipalities. The *Landrat* is the highest office of the *Kreise*. He or she may be elected by the *Kreistag* (county council), by the municipal councils, or by the population as a whole.

Although these institutions vary greatly in size and economic power, living conditions across Germany are fairly standard. This is due to the *Länder-finanzausgleich*. This is a law which commits the federal government to providing financial support to a Land if its citizens would not otherwise enjoy the same standard of living as the citizens of other Länder. Unification has made the task of ensuring equal living conditions that much harder, because some eastern Länder suffer from poor infrastructure and high unemployment.

Sources: U. Andersen u. W. Woyke, Hg., Handwörterbuch des politischen Systems der Bundesrepublik Deutschland, 2. Aufl., Opladen 1995; Erich Schmidt Verlag, Zahlenbilder 62110.

31 ELECTIONS

Germany's electoral system is a mixture of proportional representation and majority voting: personalized proportional voting. The voters elect half of all members of parliament (MPs) directly through majority voting. Such MPs could be elected by as little as 20 percent of the vote. Voters also cast a vote for the party of their choice. The other half of MPs are then chosen by the parties, from their own lists held in each Land, and based on their share of these second votes.

In the 1994-98 or 13th Bundestag there were, officially, 656 MPs, elected from 328 constituencies. In reality there were 672 MPs. This discrepancy is explained by the *Überhangmandate*, or the extra seats which parties can acquire in the shareout of second votes. Starting with the 15th Bundestag, which will be elected in 2002, the number of constituencies will be reduced to 299 and the number of MPs reduced to 598. At the same time, new boundary reforms will even out the size of the constituencies, which currently range from 152,000 to 316,000.

Another peculiarity of German voting law, the ' 5 percent clause', means that no party can enter parliament unless they gain 5 percent of the total party vote or win three direct seats. It was introduced during the 2nd Bundestag (1953-57) in an attempt to keep extremist groups from both left and right out of parliament. It was inspired by the experience of the Weimar republic (1919-33). In the 1st Bundestag (1949-53) there were MPs from as many as 11 political parties. In 1994, the PDS (*Partei des Demokratischen Sozialismus*, formerly the East German communist party) received less than 5 percent of the vote but won direct seats in four east Berlin constituencies.

Elections take place at all levels of government: the federal (Bundestag), the Länder and on the municipal and district level. Since 1979 there have been direct elections to the European Parliament every five years. Germany has 99 seats out of a total of 626.

Local elections are more likely to be determined by local issues. It is not surprising, therefore, that some cities may have an SPD mayor but vote quite differently in elections for the Landtag or Bundestag. Special interest groups (*Freie Wählergemeinschaften*) which would stand no chance in elections for the Landtag or Bundestag, often play a decisive part in municipal and district elections.

During the last twenty years the number of non voters or floating voters has greatly increased as traditional bonds to the parties, created by job, religion or education, have loosened.

There are no great differences between men and women in party preferences, but there are big differences between age groups, except in the case of the FDP. In the 1994 Bundestag elections, the CDU was least popular with women aged between 25 and 34, and most popular with women over 60. For the SPD the opposite was true. Women of all age groups are more inclined than men to vote for the Greens.

Sources: Forschungsgruppe Wahlen, Bericht Nr. 76: Bundestagswahl 1994, 2. Aufl., Mannheim 1994; G. A. Ritter u. M. Niehuss, Wahlen in Deutschland 1946-1991. Ein Handbuch, München 1991; DAS PARLAMENT vom 13./20.1.1995, S. 4.

32 POLITICAL PARTIES

Most Western democracies have only two major political parties, perhaps partly due to the system of majority voting (see note to **31. Elections**). Article 21 of Germany's Basic Law states that political parties help to form the people's political will, that they can be freely founded, and that their aims and organization should follow the democratic principles of a free society.

With the end of the Second World War came the end of the era of National Socialism and the one party dictatorship of the National Socialist German Workers' Party (*Nationalsozialistische Deutsche Arbeiterpartei* or NSDAP). After 1945, the older political parties were allowed once again, and the Christian Democratic Union (*Christlich Demokratische Union*, CDU) was founded; in Bavaria (Bayern), this is the Christian Social Union (*Christlich Soziale Union*, CSU). At first the Social Democratic Party (*Sozialdemokratische Partei Deutschlands*, SPD), which had been founded in the1860s, was very influential and in 1946 it had 600,000 members in the three western zones. The SPD was the workers' party, which had always had close ties to the trade unions. The liberal Free Democratic Party (*Freie Demokratische Partei*, FDP) was also strong. The Communist Party of Germany (*Kommunistische Partei Deutschlands*, KPD) was represented in the 1st Bundestag, but in 1956 it was prohibited by the Federal Constitutional Court. As a result of the 5 percent clause (introduced in 1953: see note to **31. Elections**), the party spectrum in West Germany was shaped by only three parties: the CDU/CSU, the SPD and the FDP. The Green Party (DIE GRÜNE, a new political party which developed largely out of the environmental movement, was first represented in the 10th Bundestag (1983-87).

After 1990, the party spectrum was affected by unification. The East German political parties, founded on Marxist-Leninist principles, needed to be integrated into the pluralist party system of West Germany. In 1946, the United German Socialist Party (*Sozialistische Deutsche Einheitspartei*, SED) had been formed in East Germany by the amalgamation of the KPD and the SPD. After unification, the SED was succeeded by the Party of Democratic Socialism (PDS) which was to become a new third force in the eastern Länder. State funding of election campaigns has been regulated by the1967 law on political parties. State funding is fundamental to the financing of political parties in Germany, though rather controversial with the general public. Any political party which achieves 5 percent of the vote (thereby enabling it to be represented in the Bundestag) receives DM5.00 per voter, regardless of whether it is perceived as being on the extreme right or left. Article 21 of the Basic Law states that parties have to declare publicly the sources and use of their funding as well as their actual wealth. Although the political parties aim to be self financing, over 50 percent of their income comes as support from the federal government. In Italy, Spain and Sweden the percentage of government support is equally high.

Extreme right and left wing parties are under particular scrutiny, both within Germany and elsewhere. Recent German history means that the right is regarded with particular suspicion. Right wing parties such as the National Democratic Party of Germany (*National-Demokratische Partei Deutschland*,NPD) in 1966-68 or the Republicans in the mid 1990s, have won a number of seats in the parliaments of individual Länder, though not in the Bundestag. Extremist parties which ignore the constitutional consensus have no chance of establishing themselves in the Länder parliaments for any length of time.

Sources: A. Mintzel u. H. Oberreuter, Hg., Parteien in der BRD, Bonn 1992; Beilage zur Wochenzeitung DAS PARLAMENT vom 17.5.1996; Bundestagsdrucksache 13/4503, Bonn 1996; Parteienzentralen: Mitteilungen aller Parteien an den Verf., Herbst 1996; Bundesministerium des Innern, Hg., Verfassungsschutzbericht, Bonn 1994.

33 POLITICAL PARTICIPATION

Dissatisfaction with roads, transport and urban planning has led to ever increasing demands for greater political participation. The result has been a growth of 'citizens' initiatives', a new concept in Germany that began in the 1960s and gained strength in the 1970s from the women's movement and the environmental movement.

The need to increase the level of democracy has become so widely accepted that at any one time about 60 percent of registered voters are willing to commit themselves to citizens' initiatives. In East Germany, a similar political culture began to develop just before unification, mainly through peace prayers in the churches and the citizens' rights movement. Since unification in 1990, the citizens' rights movement has been free to adapt to its changed circumstances.

At the local level, citizens' initiatives are mainly registered as *Vereine* (see note to **16. Clubs and Associations**). For single issues, the citizens' referendum, written into the municipal code, is the most important means of countering the power of the political system. There is a two step procedure for all referenda. Before a referendum can be held within a municipality, it must have the support of a certain percentage of all registered voters, recorded in a petition with a full list of signatures. The percentage required varies by Land and is between 25 and 50 percent of registered voters. The regulations in city states (*Stadtstaaten*) are rather different because there are no municipalities (*Gemeinden*) and they have the constitution of a Land. In the city states, and also in some Länder, a citizens' petition for a referendum can instigate changes to the law. A referendum can make changes to the law mandatory.

Citizens can influence political decisions and institutions in a number of different ways. Article 8 of the Basic Law asserts the freedom to assemble, demonstrate and congregate as part of general civil rights. Article 17 of the Basic Law asserts the rights of all citizens to petition or complain in writing to the Länder parliaments or to the Bundestag. The articles in the Länder constitutions are similar. These provisions have been used more and more frequently since the beginning of demands for greater political participation.

Parliamentary commissioners have been established on the same principle as the Swedish Ombudsman (as elsewhere in Europe). Bodies have also been set up to protect specific social groups. Since 1956, every soldier can appeal directly to a defence commissioner elected by the Bundestag for a period of five years. Data protection commissioners and women's commissioners have become established in government departments and large institutions.

In Germany, citizens' rights and the power to challenge unpopular political decisions will become more and more significant. It is these new forms of community involvement that have recently made most progress.

Sources: Bundestagsdrucksache 13/4498; Beilage zur Wochenzeitung DAS PARLAMENT, 7. Mai 1993, S. 7; infas-Repräsentativbefragung im Bundesgebiet, Juli 1995; Karlsruhe: Ausgaben der „Badischen Neuesten Nachrichten"; Amt für Stadtentwicklung, Statistik und Stadtforschung der Stadt Karlsruhe, telefonische Auskunft März 1997; W. Zapf u. R. Habich, Hg., Wohlfahrtsentwicklung im vereinten Deutschland, Berlin 1996, S. 298.

34 SOCIAL MOVEMENTS

From its beginning, industrial and civil society has been shaped by social movements, some of which eventually grew into political parties, associations, or other public bodies. Such movements have included the workers' movement, the Christian social movement, the women's movement, the youth movement, and reform movements – plus the free spirits, liberals, friends of nature and many others. All these movements saw themselves as flexible and unbureaucratic, dynamic and forward looking, and serving directly the interests of the people as a whole or of specific social groups.

The peace movement and anti nuclear movement were important precursors of the new social movements that have grown up since the 1960s, when events and circumstances brought them to a wider audience. The student movement, which included teachers, grammar school pupils, apprentices and many more groups, was particularly important, as were the subsequent communes and experiments in alternative ways of living. From the mid 1960s, citizens' initiatives (see note to **33. Political Participation**) also widened the spectrum and increased acceptance of social movements. A comprehensive change in values took place. This can be described as a moving away from traditional and materialistic values of duty, work and achievement, towards other values of self realization, individualism, social participation and hedonism.

The failures of the student movement paved the way for a multitude of alternative movements. Since the early 1970s, increasing destruction of natural resources on a worldwide basis has led to one of the most important of these, the environmental movement. The Green List Environmental Protection (*Grüne Liste Umwelt-schutz*) attracted most members. It signalled changing values and new ways of global thinking and networking. Today, the BUND (Association for the Protection of the Environment and Nature) and Greenpeace are among the most widely known environmental groups. From the 1970s onwards, the Green Party (DIE GRÜNEN) established itself in municipal and district councils and helped to bring about a range of new institutions and legislation.

The women's movement has also prompted new institutions and initiatives: women's refuges, women's commissioners, commissioners for equality, research on women, numerous legal initiatives in all areas, and a multitude of social and cultural offerings such as women's cafes, and cultural and educational centres.

The Greens illustrate one of the dilemmas of all social movements, so far unresolved. By becoming an institution and forming a political party (a federal party was formed in 1980) have they introduced hierarchies, bureaucratization and nepotism, the very concepts formerly deemed to hinder social and political change? Or is lasting political success dependent on such a process? The debate between the 'Fundis' (fundamentalists of the movement) and the 'Realos' (party political realists) exemplifies this dilemma.

Sources: H. Klages, Werte und Wertewandel, in: B. Schäfers u. W. Zapf, Hg., Handwörterbuch zur Gesellschaft Deutschlands, Opladen 1997; H. Meulemann, Werte und Wertewandel. Zur Identität einer geteilten und wieder vereinten Nation, Weinheim, München 1996; R. Roth u. D. Rucht, Hg., Neue soziale Bewegungen in der Bundesrepublik Deutschland, 2. Aufl, Bonn 1990. Einzelne Informationen: Bund für Umwelt und Naturschutz e. V. (BUND), Bundesgeschäftsstelle, Mitteilungen, Bonn 1996; Bundesministerium für Familie, Senioren, Frauen u. Jugend, Hg., Aufstellung über die Förderung von Frauenhäusern in den Bundesländern, Bonn 1996; Greenpeace e. V., Mitteilungen und Informationsbroschüren; DIE ZEIT v. 28.2.1997.

35 EUROPEAN UNITY

The European Union, which in 1998 has 15 member states, has its roots in the European Coal and Steel Community. Founded in 1951 by the Treaty of Paris, its main purpose was to pool coal and steel resources in order to avoid the danger of further war in Europe. Its members were Belgium, France, West Germany, Italy, Luxembourg and the Netherlands. In 1957, these same six countries signed two Treaties of Rome, founding the European Economic Community (EEC) and the European Atomic Energy Community (Euratom). The aim of the EEC was to establish a common market and to bring about a gradual convergence in the economic policies of member states. In 1965, the three organizations were placed under a joint umbrella. In 1967 a joint Council of Ministers was set up and a joint European Commission began sitting in Brussels.

As a result of the unification of Germany in 1990, East Germany's five new Länder became part of the Federal Republic of Germany and Germany became entitled to 18 additional seats in the European Parliament (see also **31. Elections**). The European Parliament (its official name since 1987) sits in Strasbourg and Brussels. Since 1979, Members of the European Parliament (MEPs) have been directly elected by the populations of member states. MEPs of different political parties group together in factions of similar political interests. The rights of the European Parliament are still very limited. The Council of Ministers and the Commission, the most important executive bodies in the European Union, are thereby very strong. This may also explain why only 57 percent of the electorate turned out to vote in the 1994 elections.

In the Treaty on European Union, signed in Maastricht in 1992, the member states confirmed their commitment to political union. As a counterbalance, the interests of individual member states and their regions were strengthened by the setting up of a new Committee of the Regions and by introducing the principle of subsidiarity. The concept of subsidiarity stems from Christian social ethics, and means that problems should be solved, wherever possible, at the level at which they arise. The larger government entity (Land, nation state, or the European Union itself) can only take action when the smaller entity has exhausted its capacity.

The EU budget is controversial. In 1995, Germany's share was 22.3 billion Ecus, out of a total of 76 billion. The main source of finance is a 1.4 percent share of each member state's Value Added Tax (sales tax). About half the EU budget is spent on agriculture and about a third goes into financial support for poorer EU countries. Since unification in 1990 Germany has been a beneficiary.

Over the next few years, the introduction of economic and monetary union (EMU) and a common currency, the Euro, will dominate European politics. In 1998 it will be decided which member states will participate. This will not only depend on their willingness to do so, but on whether they have been able to meet strict financial criteria fixed at Maastricht. As of 1 January 1999, the exchange rates of those countries will be fixed and the Euro will be introduced for cashless transactions. On 1 January 2002, Euro banknotes and coins will be introduced and on 1 July 2002, former national currencies will become invalid.

Enlargement of the EU is also under debate. Switzerland, which has been surrounded by EU countries since Austria became a member in 1995, cannot put its application for membership forward without agreement in a referendum.

Sources: St. Hradil u. St. Immerfall, Hg., Die westeuropäischen Gesellschaften im Vergleich, Opladen 1997; J. Monar, N. Neuwahl, P. Noack, Hg., Sachwörterbuch zur Europäischen Union, Stuttgart 1993; Allensbacher Archiv, IfD-Umfragen 6020 und 3276 (Mai 1996 / Juni 1996); Globus Nr. 2642/1996, Nr. 3680/1996, Nr. 3824/1996; DIE ZEIT v. 8.11.1996; Spiegel-Dokumentation Europa, Daten. Fakten. Trends. Hamburg 1993.